Life
CONQUERS
Death

Life CONQUERS Death

Meditations on the Garden, the Cross, and the Tree of Life

John Arnold

ZONDERVAN®

ZONDERVAN.com/
AUTHORTRACKER
follow your favorite authors

We want to hear from you. Please send your comments about this book to us in care of zreview@zondervan.com. Thank you.

Life Conquers Death
Copyright © 2007 by John Arnold

Requests for information should be addressed to:
Zondervan, *Grand Rapids, Michigan 49530*

Library of Congress Cataloging-in-Publication Data

Arnold, John, 1933 –
    Life conquers death : meditations on the garden, the cross, and the tree of life /
John Arnold.
       p.   cm.
    Includes bibliographical references.
    ISBN-13: 978-0-310-27976-1
    ISBN-10: 0-310-27976-3
    1. Lent – Meditations. I. Title.
BV85.A76   2007
242'.34 – dc22   2007019928

Interior design by Beth Shagene

Printed in the United States of America

---

07 08 09 10 11 12 • 23 22 21 20 19 18 17 16 15 14 13 12 11 10 9 8 7 6 5 4 3 2

Contents

Foreword

John Arnold once said that he had learned Russian during his military service as part of a process of equipping him for conflict during the Cold War era; but what his knowledge of Russian had done was to equip him instead for a lifetime of friendship and understanding. He had never, he said, uttered a word of Russian in anger. It is an apt parable for the way in which God overrules human suspicion and human conflict to draw his own purposes gently through.

This book is the fruit of a long absorption in the riches of the Christian tradition, East and West, and its subject matter is nothing less than the great central theme of redemption, treated with a fullness of classical theological sensitivity. But it also represents that lifetime of listening to and loving the heritage of Russia in particular — the great twentieth-century testimonies to hope and human dignity out of the heart of terrible suffering. Writers like Pasternak and Solzhenitsyn show, without any evasion or sentimentality, how the beauty of the human face can show itself in the most apparently inhuman of places. John Arnold's superb meditations on these stories and testimonies lead directly into meditation on the gospel narratives that lie behind them and make full sense of them.

God has chosen to redeem us and restore our humanity by nothing less than his own journey into the wars and gulags and inner mental prisons where human beings try to blot out the image of God in themselves and each other. The face of glory has to be allowed to come to light in the heart of the darkness. If it were only a slightly improved version of the best we can do, we should have no compelling reason to see it as God's face. But when it appears in the depth of greatest despair and inhumanity, it shows its true and indestructible power.

With that vision in our hearts and minds, we can, as John Arnold urges, take up again the task of humanising our own environment — our built environment with all its social tragedies and traumas, but also our whole material environment, symbolised in these pages by the recurring image of the tree of life.

This book is a powerful statement of basic Christian hope; I asked John to write it after hearing him deliver two retreats in which I felt that I had been introduced afresh, with authority and profundity, to what was most central in our faith. I hope many others will find here just that sense of hearing great and supposedly familiar truths as if for the first time.

+ROWAN CANTUAR:
Archbishop of Canterbury
Lambeth Palace, London
Visit of the Blessed Virgin Mary to Elizabeth, 2007

Acknowledgements

M y chief thanks go to the Archbishop of Canterbury for his kind invitation to produce his Lent Book for 2008, for his encouragement to proceed with the work and for his gracious Foreword.

Next I would like to thank my daughter, Frances, for reading the entire manuscript with critical and appreciative care. Any remaining errors and lapses are my own.

Mrs Jill Pollock typed several drafts with diligence and cheerfulness. The editors and staff of Zondervan have been generous with their time, their advice, their expertise and their professionalism. I am grateful to them all.

Much of the material is based on addresses, meditations and sermons, delivered over several decades and not originally intended for publication. In many cases it is not possible to identify the source of a particular phrase or insight. I am, therefore, indebted to innumerable anonymous persons, living and departed, for their conversation, their writings, their teaching and their inspiration. Parts of chapters 3–7 have appeared in 'Theology' and 'Sobornost' and in the Proceedings of the British-Russian Conferences on Religion and Literature, Durham and Moscow, 2000–2004.

Chapters 5 and 6 contain substantial quotations from *Dr Zhivago* by Boris Pasternak, published by Harvill Press. They are reprinted by kind permission of the Random House Group Ltd.

The translations of Pasternak's poems and of Solzhenitsyn's prayer are my own. For my translation and abridgement of the passage from *The Devils* at the beginning of chapter 2, I consulted *The Possessed* by Fyodor Dostoyevsky, translated by Andrew MacAndrew (Signet Classics, 1962).

I would like to thank Cambridge University Press for permission to quote from *Pasternak* by Henry Gifford (1977) and Stainer & Bell Ltd for permission to quote the hymn 'It Was on a Friday Morning' by Sydney Carter. I am also grateful to The Pierpont Morgan Library / Art Resource in New York for their permission to use *The Three Crosses* etching by Rembrandt.

Scriptural references are, unless otherwise indicated, taken from the New Revised Standard Version (copyright 1989 Division of Christian Education of the National Council of Churches of Christ in the United States of America), with the exception of quotations from the Psalms, for which I have preferred the familiar cadences of the Book of Common Prayer.

Finally, I would like to thank my wife, Anneliese, for her constant support and stimulating companionship, not just during the writing of this book but throughout nearly fifty years of life together.

CANTERBURY
Trinty Sunday 2007

Preface

'The Preface is the first and also the last thing in a book,' wrote Michael Lermontov for the second edition of *A Hero of Our Time* in 1841. It comes first, though it is written last, to explain the structure and to guide the reader.

Like Lermontov's novel, this book is made up of a number of disparate elements, composed on various occasions over many years and rewritten for coherence and for ease of use as a Lent Book. It has no one plot or single theme; but it does have a rough chronological framework based on the Bible and it is unified by the constant presence of a hero, not only of our time but of all time, Jesus Christ.

Each chapter is complete in itself and may be read as such. Study group leaders might choose to take two chapters a week during Lent, or, alternatively, to concentrate either on chapters 8 to 12, which are conventional Lenten fare, or on chapters 3 to 7, which are similar to one another but rather different from the rest of the book. They might also wish to choose a verse or a prayer from the text, together with lots of silence, as aids to reflection.

The central section (chapters 3–7) requires some explanation. Ever since I was trained as an interpreter in the army in the Joint Services School for Linguists (see Geoffrey Elliott and Harold Shukman, *Secret Classrooms: An Untold Story of the Cold War* [London: St Ermin's Press, 2002]), the Russian language and Russian literature have been companions in my life, which they have enriched and transformed. They have been useful in my work 'behind the Iron Curtain', as we used to say, and in the Conference of European Churches; but, beyond that, they broadened and deepened my faith and have been constant sources of pleasure, wisdom, challenge and consolation.

My first loves were the great nineteenth-century masters (see page 88). By the mid-twentieth century it seemed as if that great tradition had been crushed to death by the imposition of Socialist Realism upon all art forms in the Soviet Union. The sudden and unexpected re-emergence of the Russian novel as the bearer of the great themes of life and love, faith and hope, in the works of Pasternak and Solzhenitsyn was itself a parable of resurrection. I have sought to integrate what I have learnt from these authors with what I understand of the gospel; and I shall be well satisfied if I send readers back to their books as well as to the Bible. It is from Solzhenitsyn's apologia for his own work that I have taken the title *Life Conquers Death, and the past is overcome by the future.*

A common factor in all chapters, and one that has guided me in the choice of material, is the presence of wood and trees, either in reality or as metaphors. Perhaps that is not surprising, given the centrality of the cross, both as a real, tangible, material object and also as an imperishable symbol of our faith. I toyed with the possibility of using this recurring theme as the framework and title of the book, but decided against imposing an artificial unity onto the material. Similarly I have left the contemporary ecological implications largely implicit; but, like a Russian peasant begging forgiveness of the earth he was about to plough, I would like to ask pardon of the trees which have died that this book might live.

CHAPTER 1

The Tree of the Knowledge of Good and Evil

Creation and Fall

In the day that the Lord *God made the earth and the heavens, when no plant of the field was yet in the earth and no herb of the field had yet sprung up – for the* Lord *God had not caused it to rain upon the earth, and there was no one to till the ground; but a stream would rise from the earth, and water the whole face of the ground – then the* Lord *God formed man from the dust of the ground, and breathed into his nostrils the breath of life; and the man became a living being. And the* Lord *God planted a garden in Eden, in the east; and there he put the man whom he had formed. Out of the ground the* Lord *God made to grow every tree that is pleasant to the sight and good for food, the tree of life also in the midst of the garden, and the tree of the knowledge of good and evil...*

The Lord *God took the man and put him in the garden of Eden to till it and keep it. And the* Lord *God commanded the man, 'You may freely eat of every tree of the garden; but of the tree of the knowledge of good and evil you shall not eat, for in the day that you eat of it you shall die.'*

Then the Lord *God said, 'It is not good that the man should be alone; I will make him a helper as his partner.' So* out of the ground the LORD God formed every animal of the field and every bird of the air, and brought them to the man to see what he would call them; and whatever the man called every living creature, that was its name. The man gave names to all cattle, and to the birds of the air, and to every animal of the field; but for the man there was not found a helper as his partner. So the LORD God caused a deep sleep to fall upon the man, and he slept; then he took one of his ribs and closed up its place with flesh. And the rib that the LORD God had taken from the man he made into a woman and brought her to the man. Then the man said,

'This at last is bone of my bones
 and flesh of my flesh;
this one shall be called Woman,
 for out of Man this one was taken.'

Therefore a man leaves his father and his mother and clings to his wife, and they become one flesh. And the man and his wife were both naked, and were not ashamed.

Now the serpent was more crafty than any other wild animal that the LORD God had made. He said to the woman, 'Did God say, "You shall not eat from any tree in the garden"?' The woman said to the serpent, 'We may eat of the fruit of the trees in the garden; but God said, "You shall not eat of the fruit of the tree that is in the middle of the garden, nor shall you touch it, or you shall die."' But the serpent said to the woman, 'You will not die; for God knows that when you eat of it your eyes will be opened, and you will be like God, knowing good and evil.' So when the woman saw that the tree was good for food, and that it was a delight to the eyes, and that the tree was to be desired to make one wise, she took of its fruit and ate; and she also gave some to her husband, who was with her, and he ate. Then the eyes of both were opened, and they knew that they were naked; and they sewed fig leaves together and made loincloths for themselves.

They heard the sound of the LORD God walking in the garden at the time of the evening breeze, and the man and his wife hid themselves from the presence of the LORD God among the trees of the garden. But the LORD God called to the man, and said to him, 'Where are you?' He said, 'I heard the sound of you in the garden, and I was afraid, because I was naked; and I hid myself.' He said, 'Who told you that you were naked? Have you eaten from the tree of which I commanded you not to eat?' The man said, 'The woman whom you gave to be with me, she gave me fruit from the tree, and I ate.' Then the LORD God said to the woman, 'What is this that you have done?' The woman said, 'The serpent tricked me, and I ate.' The LORD God said to the serpent,

> 'Because you have done this,
>> cursed are you among all animals
>> and among all wild creatures;
> upon your belly you shall go,
>> and dust you shall eat
>> all the days of your life.
> I will put enmity between you and the woman,
>> and between your offspring and hers;
> he will strike your head,
>> and you will strike his heel.'

To the woman he said,

> 'I will greatly increase your pangs in childbearing;
>> in pain you shall bring forth children,
> yet your desire shall be for your husband,
>> and he shall rule over you.'

And to the man he said,

> *'Because you have listened to the voice of your wife,*
> > *and have eaten of the tree*
> *about which I commanded you,*
> > *"You shall not eat of it,"*
> *cursed is the ground because of you;*
> > *in toil you shall eat of it all the days of your life;*
> *thorns and thistles it shall bring forth for you;*
> > *and you shall eat the plants of the field.*
> *By the sweat of your face*
> > *you shall eat bread*
> *until you return to the ground,*
> > *for out of it you were taken;*
> *you are dust,*
> > *and to dust you shall return.'*

The man named his wife Eve, because she was the mother of all living. And the LORD God made garments of skins for the man and for his wife, and clothed them.

Then the LORD God said, 'See, the man has become like one of us, knowing good and evil; and now, he might reach out his hand and take also from the tree of life, and eat, and live forever' – therefore the LORD God sent him forth from the garden of Eden, to till the ground from which he was taken. He drove out the man; and at the east of the garden of Eden he placed the cherubim, and a sword flaming and turning to guard the way to the tree of life. (Genesis 2:4–9; 2:15–3:24)

A favourite cartoon of mine shows a serpent in the Garden of Eden twisting round a tree and whispering in Eve's ear: 'Play your cards right and I can get you onto page three of the Bible.' I invite you to look in your Bibles at Genesis 2, and there on page 3 is Eve, except that here she is simply called 'the woman'. Being called Eve, the mother of all living, comes later after the story of the fall, in which she, unlike Adam, is anonymous.

That is only one of many oddities about this story, which, perhaps more than any other since the dawn of time and of consciousness, has haunted the imagination and furnished with imagery the minds of men and women seeking to make sense of the human condition and to answer questions like: Why does everything go wrong? – indeed, Why does anything go wrong? What is the peculiar position of humankind in the scheme of things and what are our responsibilities? Why, unlike the animals, do we feel shame and wear clothes? Why are the sexes so strongly attracted to each other? Why do women put up with men and why is childbearing so painful? Why do we fear snakes and find them loathsome? Why do we blame each other when things go wrong? Why are we always on the move? And, finally, what shall we say when God asks, 'Where are you?'

The answers, in so far as there are any, are given not in the form of a treatise, or a formula, or a code, but a story – a special kind of story, technically called a myth. I say 'technically' because in everyday speech the word 'myth' is taken to mean an untrue historical story, whereas its real meaning is a true non-historical story. It tells the truth in narrative form, just as poetry or drama or the tales from the *Arabian Nights* do, in a way which is at once psychologically profound, economical in form and above all memorable. The problem is that we tend to remember selectively; and this story has often been misused as primarily teaching, for example, the origin of clothing, the relationship between men and women or the role of sex in the transmission of sin. Such uses of this story rob it of its real power and inner truthfulness.

Of man's first disobedience, and the fruit
Of that forbidden tree, whose mortal taste
Brought death into the world and all our woe
With loss of Eden, till one greater Man
Restore us, and regain the blissful seat,
Sing heavenly Muse.

That is Milton, not me; and just as I began by saying 'Open the Bible at page 3 and read on', now I say 'Open *Paradise Lost* at page 1 and read what Milton actually wrote, rather than what you might think he wrote.'

Note that Milton, right at the start of his epic, before even depicting the primeval chaos which itself preceded creation, looks forward already to the 'one greater Man' (with a capital M) so that the possibility of redemption predates captivity, and the antidote to sin and death is prescribed before anyone has fallen ill or contracted the fatal malady. So also, in Genesis this story does not end without the prediction that a descendent of Eve will strike at the serpent's head. That passage may be taken as hinting at a pre-existent Son, the Word who was with the Father before the world was made, by whom the world was made and who, in the fullness of time, was sent not to condemn the world but that the world might be saved (John 3:17). Cut into the apple of the Bible at any point and it will always disclose this pattern; the story of our fall is inseparable from the story, not only of our creation, but also of our salvation.

The Gospels do not mention Adam and Eve and the serpent in the Garden of Eden, and nor do any New Testament writers except St Paul, and then only fleetingly, not to explain sin or recount the fall but to insist on the unity of the human race first in Adam and in mortality, then in Christ, whom he calls the last Adam, and in the resurrection.

Perhaps most surprisingly, Jesus in his recorded utterances never once mentions Adam or refers to this story. He, and with him the whole New Testament, pays little attention to the account of sin in Genesis 3; but he takes for granted and as common ground the psychological and theological account in the story of Noah in Genesis 6:5 and 11, 'every inclination of the thoughts of their hearts was only evil continually,' and 'The earth was corrupt in God's sight, and the earth was filled with violence.' Thus, for example, we find Jesus teaching his disciples, 'It is from within, from the human heart, that evil intentions come: fornication, theft, murder, adultery, avarice … these evil things come from within, and they defile a person' (Mark 7:21–23). The disadvantage of these profound insights of Genesis 6, even when retold by Jesus, is that they come to us as a statement, followed by a list, so that they do not form images in the mind; they are thus less memorable than the parables of Jesus and the picturesque story in Genesis 3.

The point about forming images in the mind is where we approach the heart of the mystery and the beginning of the answer to the psalmist's question, 'What are human beings?' (Psalm 8:4). On page 2 of the Bible, in a different story, it is said, 'God created humankind in his image, in the image of God he created them; male and female he created them' (Genesis 1:27). Men and women are creatures, like everything else in the universe; but uniquely they are in the image of God.

What does this mean? Certainly not that any of our faces is like the face of God so that he could be picked out in an identity parade – at least not until the coming of Jesus and the development of icons, which is another story. Almost certainly the image of God means upright posture. Men and women are God-like when they stand up and stand tall – *homo erectus*. This brings enormous advantages and some disadvantages. It would take an anthropologist to catalogue them all. One of the advantages is that men and women became immensely more attractive to each other, capable of bonding in more inventive and intricate ways, *homo ludens*; one of the disadvantages is that they need clothing not only to cope with extremes of heat and cold but also to simultaneously enhance and subdue their beauty, *homo pudens*.

Upright posture makes us more vulnerable to pain and suffering and to 'the thousand natural shocks that flesh is heir to'.[1] The narrow pelvis, which makes possible walking on two legs, also makes childbearing difficult, dangerous and painful (Genesis 3:16); and we are liable to backache, especially if we till the soil (Genesis 3:19); but we can set against that the freeing of the hands for making and using tools – *homo habilis*.

It is also along these lines that some of the questions 'Why?' may be answered. The most important consequence of upright posture, however, was that it made possible the enlargement of the central nervous system, a large brain, with capacities far in excess of anything else in the universe, not only in quantity but also in quality. Conscious thought, imaginative thought, the ability to make images or pictures in the mind, to think God's thoughts after him, and to be loving, creative, spontaneous and free – this is to be human, gloriously and uniquely human in the image of God, *homo sapiens*.

Like upright posture, the human brain brings its own problems with it. No matter where you go, you find human sin; theologians speak of the 'universality' of sin. To be free to think good thoughts is to be free to think evil thoughts; and the immense advances in skill and cunning, in co-operation and adaptability, which enabled humankind to become such a successful species and colonise the whole globe, are precisely the disadvantages which we now see everywhere at work. The human ability to master nature and dominate every other living thing has turned into the ability to destroy nature and exploit every other living thing.

The fall is not just something which happened long ago, in the beginning, in Genesis, in the Garden of Eden. The fall is happening now, in the historic present, all over the world, in every aspect of individual and corporate life, in the relationships between men and women, humankind and nature, humankind and God. It is now that the Lord sees that the wickedness of humankind is great in the earth and that 'every inclination of the thoughts of their hearts is only evil continually'; it is now that 'the earth is corrupt in God's sight and full of violence'. We have only to read the newspapers or watch television or, better still, look inward into our own hearts and minds, to be acutely conscious of the consequences 'of man's first disobedience and the fruit of that forbidden tree'.

One of the most remarkable changes in general attitudes over the past 100 years – and especially in the past 20 or 30 – has been in our view of human beings and their relationship to the world. A hundred years ago many, perhaps most, sensitive and educated people were appalled at the apparent wastefulness and indifferent cruelty of nature – 'nature red in tooth and claw'[2] – while being generally optimistic about humankind and its capacity for progress through the application of industry and science. Now the great-grandchildren of those sensitive and educated people are appalled by the wastefulness and indifferent cruelty of human beings, while being more than ever appreciative of the economy and efficiency of nature and of the natural environment that sustains life.

The picture which is sketched in the first chapters of Genesis is not a scientific account of the origin of species in the past, but it does seem to fit our experience of life on earth today. That is not surprising. As Joseph Butler wrote in *The Analogy of Religion*,

'Nature and scripture tell the same story, God Himself being the author of both.'

'Out of the ground the LORD God made to grow every tree that is pleasant to the sight and good for food, the tree of life also in the midst of the garden, and the tree of the knowledge of good and evil' (Genesis 2:9). The world is a paradise or enclosed garden, that is to say, with great wonders and delights but also with limits. Within those limits there is everything anyone could possibly want: abundant resources for body, mind and spirit, 'trees pleasant to look at and good for food', so long as humankind tends them, cares for them and helps them on to a greater perfection. We can make the desert blossom like a rose, we can farm the seas and the dry land, we can fashion cities to dwell in – everything in the garden can be lovely.

But that is not the whole story. The world as we know it falls short of its potential; it has fallen through us. Only we among all the creatures can and do destroy our own and others' habitat, only we can and do jeopardise the biosphere, only we can and do produce paradise lost, turning the place of life into a place of death. (There is added poignancy now in the thought that the writer of Genesis 2 seems to have assumed that the garden of Eden was situated at the confluence of the Tigris and the Euphrates in present-day Iraq.)

'The LORD God took the man and put him in the garden of Eden to till it and keep it' (Genesis 2:15). Certainly Genesis 1:26–28 speaks of humankind having dominion over the earth and all living creatures. But we are becoming increasingly aware of the fact that the basic task is to tend the ecology, to look after it rather than exploit it. The biggest single change in theology in my lifetime has been the adoption by the churches of the ecological agenda. Whether that is too late remains to be seen.

Just as creation is not only a point of departure in the past, but an activity of God in the present, so is the fall of Adam and Eve not just something that they did once in the garden of Eden, but is a permanent feature of human life today in which we are all involved. Almost all the ecological damage to our planet has been done in my lifetime. The people of this generation will have something to answer for at the day of judgement, as God himself says to Adam after the fall: 'Cursed is the ground because of you' (Genesis 3:17). To us has been given the privilege of understanding what that means and implies, really as well as symbolically. There is a terrifying verse in the book of Revelation, too, which reads: '[Now is] the time ... for destroying those who destroy the earth' (Revelation 11:18).

In our lifetime the symbolic has become real in other ways, so that, for example, in unlocking nuclear energy in explosive form we have become the angel with the flaming sword preventing ourselves from ever recapturing our innocence. And when the symbolic becomes real, then we know that we are living in what the Bible calls the last days or the end, for we experience creation, fall, nature, history and judgement, Alpha and Omega, the beginning and the end, not as a succession of events – though it is only as a succession of events that they can be set out in a book – but as a single complex experience, the life of humankind under God. Men and women of faith perceive within that, not only judgement but also mercy, not only loss but also redemption, not only fall but also rising again because for them the story is not only the story of humankind in Adam; it is also the story of humankind in Christ.

Now there is something else which has also changed dramatically over the past hundred years, and especially in the years since the Second World War, and that is the increase in knowledge. It is only comparatively recently that we have acquired the art of using the scientific method to increase the rate at which we increase knowledge. One of the things we have done, like a child discovering what can be done with a box of matches, is to give ourselves a fright, comparable to the fright which Palaeolithic man gave himself when he discovered sex and violence and which Neolithic man gave himself when he invented agriculture and civilisation, and developed religion in order to help him cope with life as it now had to be lived, with his eyes open and his loins girded, outside paradise, east of Eden, full of the knowledge of good and evil. It is tempting for us, like Adam, to blame God for putting the tree in the garden at all. But that is a hopeless attitude to take and one that inevitably leads to censorship, suppression and repression, to the defeat of the human spirit and to despair. God has another solution in Christ.

For Adam and Eve did not fall through acquiring knowledge any more than we do. They fell through disobedience; and then they acquired knowledge before they were ready for it. The problem with Adam and Eve, as with us, is not that they were knowledgeable but that they were precocious. Their partial knowledge of haphazard and unrelated 'facts' outstripped their maturity; and they became clever before they became wise – as is shown by that picturesque little incident of the fig leaves (Genesis 3:7). They discovered their bodies, as every succeeding generation has done, with a mixture of delight and shame, before they had the personal maturity and the developed all-round relationship to enable them to cope with this astonishing revelation.

God had not placed the tree in the garden as a test or trick to keep knowledge from them forever. A God who would do that would be a tyrant and an irrational jealous ogre – not the God and Father of our Lord Jesus Christ. God was going to add to all his mercies in creation, he was going to complete them, by giving Adam and Eve the fruit of knowledge himself, when it was ripe and they were mature, so that they should not only enjoy everything in the garden and each other but also know what it was they were enjoying and who was the giver of it. The tragedy is that they did not trust him enough to wait. In the morning they clutched and stuffed themselves on unripe fruit, while they were adolescent, before they had even explored the garden or come to appreciate what they had been given.

That is the first act in the tragicomedy of the so-called consumer society. They did not know that God was going to come to them in the cool of the evening, not to withhold anything from them but to give them the knowledge of good and evil himself and, much more than that, to give them 'his presence and his very self'.[3] Why did he come in the cool of the evening if not to speak with them and tell them stories and parables of nature and open their eyes and share their lives so that they could share his? It was, after all, just what he was prevented from doing in Eden, which he came to do later in the synagogue at Capernaum, in all the towns and villages of Galilee and on the road to Emmaus.

But the ears of Adam and Eve, which must be open in the morning if they are to be able to receive the fullness of knowledge and wisdom in the evening, are reached first by a serpentine tissue of half truths – gossip and innuendo masquerading as fact. 'Did God say, "You shall not eat from any tree in the garden"?' (Genesis 3:1). It isn't true, in fact it is almost the opposite of the truth, that God has forbidden them to eat from *any* tree in the Garden, only from one and for a little while. He had not even forbidden them to eat of the tree of life. As for death, we have absolutely no idea what death would be like without sin. I think, but I do not know, that it would be like falling asleep after a good day's work, which is what Leonardo da Vinci hoped for. What we do know, contrary to the assurances of the snake, is combined sin-and-death, which is the fruit not of the tree of knowledge but of disobedience.

In Genesis, in the beginning, in principle, Adam and Eve disobey in the morning, sin and are naked under the noonday sun; and when God comes in the evening he finds not companionship but a guilty conscience and mutual recrimination and self-justification and reproach ('the woman whom you gave to be with me'); and the long centuries of sin and suffering and of our apprenticeship in being human begin.

So God has to come again in the fullness of time in Jesus to visit and redeem his people. In the infancy and youth of Jesus, God and man recapitulate the right way to mature, to learn the disciplines of human life and to lay up the treasures of wisdom and knowledge. In paganism, gods came straight down from heaven already formed, and Pallas Athene is said to have sprung fully armed from the head of Zeus. But God – the only true God – takes the natural way; he enters the world as we do, through the womb. He *grows* in those hidden years between birth and the age of about thirty, of which a few verses in Luke's Gospel (Luke 2:41 – 52) are the only record, and he departs as we do through the grave and gate of death in order to be with us forever by resurrection and ascension.

What Jesus knew on earth, he learnt on earth, just as we do. First from Mary his mother he learnt love and language and then, from Joseph the carpenter, how to make things, how to fashion a yoke to fit easily and lighten the burden, how to create and how to mend what was broken. He also learnt, partly at home and partly in the synagogue at Nazareth, to know and love the stories and the psalms and the prophesies of the Hebrew Scriptures and to be able to apply their contents to his own day and eventually in a unique way to himself. These things he learnt from the village rabbi – one of the great unknown and unsung heroes of faith. Jesus must have had in childhood, as so many outstanding men and women have done, a teacher of rare quality. Zeffirelli, in his film *Jesus of Naza-*

reth, was right to give a few glimpses of the village rabbi of Nazareth preparing his pupils to become, at the age of about 12, Bar Mitzvah or sons of the law, preparing them to take responsibility for their own further religious life under the law.

There was a time when it was customary to present Jesus as a rough, unlettered, horny-handed son of toil. It is understandable why people, reacting against too limited and too intellectual a form of religion, should have done so. But it is a mistaken view. It is clear from the Gospels that Jesus had mastered the Scriptures – that is to say, the entire classical literature of his nation – in Hebrew, which bore the same sort of relationship to the Aramaic which he spoke as Old Norse does to English. When he went into the synagogue, he could find the Hebrew Scriptures open at any place and read off an extempore translation into Aramaic. Running translation from a written text is one of the most difficult skills to master and one which requires skilled teaching.

More than that, Jesus could then go to the very heart of what the passage meant. Formally in the synagogue and informally in impromptu debate and conversation and in discussion with his disciples, Jesus shows a unique combination of respect for what we call the Old Testament with complete mastery over it, and that to such an astonishing degree that the early Christians soon came to identify him, rather than the written scrolls, with the Word of God.

Apart from being at home in Hebrew and Aramaic, he almost certainly knew at least some Greek. It is unlikely that when he spoke with Pilate, they would have used any other language. And it would have been impossible for him to have answered Pilate in the simple, dignified and profound way he did, if he had not been, not only educated but also wise, so wise indeed that again the early Christians like St Paul simply identified him with 'the wisdom of God'. That is what Paul calls him in his first letter to the Corinthians – 'the power of God and the wisdom of God' (1 Corinthians 1:24). Wisdom, like all the good things which are eternal in heaven with God, grows slowly and matures quietly on earth among us.

Jesus grew up from baby to child, from boy to man, as we do, advancing in wisdom, though more perfectly than we do, by finding the best teachers, asking them questions and listening to the answers, and by accepting during his infancy the authority of his earthly parents, not blindly, but as the method of discipleship which alone can produce a Master. Jesus in the temple was curious, not precocious. There was nothing of the infant prodigy about him, just man growing in the image of God. He knew, unlike Adam and Eve and other sinners, how to wait for the fruit of the tree of knowledge, plucking only when both he and it were ripe.

What was the secret of this sense of timing? It was the ability born of trust in God and confidence in his own mission to look in long perspectives, beyond immediate pleasure or profit, beyond appearances and through the snake, the ability, as the letter to the Hebrews puts it, to see, as seeing the invisible (Hebrews 11:27). In this incident in his infancy, when he looked at the temple and beyond it to the dwelling place of God, when he looked at the rabbis and the written scrolls and beyond them to wisdom and the inner meaning of the law, he was beginning that process of looking at and through men and women and beyond the traditions of men to what God had ordained in Genesis, in the beginning. He was beginning that process which was to lead in a fallen world to Calvary – and beyond.

It is after Christ's victory on the cross, lifted up in the place which pious speculation assigns to the tree where Adam fell, that Paul can write to the early Christians that he wants 'their hearts to be encouraged and united in love, so that they may have all the riches of assured understanding and have the knowledge of God's mystery, that is, Christ himself' (Colossians 2:1–2). He goes on to say something which Adam should have heard and heeded in the morning, 'See to it that no one takes you captive through philosophy and empty deceit, according to human tradition, according to the elemental spirits of the universe, and not according to Christ' (Colossians 2:8). And finally, he says something which surpasses anything which Adam could have grasped BC, before Christ, and which is both my firm belief and also my earnest hope and prayer for you: 'In him the whole fullness of deity dwells bodily, and you have come to fullness in him' (Colossians 2:9–10a).

QUESTIONS

1. (a) What is your own best experience of awe and wonder at the creation?

   (b) What are the consequences for us of the belief that human beings are the one part of the visible creation which is capable of responding with praise and thanksgiving to the Creator?

   (c) Compose a short prayer or a poem or verse of a hymn on the theme of creation.

2. What are the consequences for us of the belief that every one of our fellow human beings is made in the image of God?

3. What are the consequences for us of the belief that human beings have been put on the earth in order to tend it and care for it?

4. What are the advantages and disadvantages of transmitting the doctrine of the fall as a story?

5. (a) 'Clever but not wise.' Is this a fair description of contemporary human beings?

   (b) If so, do current educational policies help or hinder the pursuit of wisdom?

CHAPTER 2

The Crib and the Crossing of Boundaries

Incarnation and Ministry

THE INCARNATION IN WORDS

It is difficult for us to get at the reality of the birth of Christ. The event has become so overgrown with holly and ivy that it may seem to be as far from our ordinary everyday lives as is the Sleeping Beauty or any other fairy story. And that is tragic, because it was precisely in order to come right into ordinary lives, to speak to us words we can understand, to live our lives with us, that God in Jesus Christ took human nature in the real womb of a real woman and became Immanuel – God with us.

That is where artists, musicians and writers come to our aid, open our eyes and help us to see. I want to share something which, more than anything else, has helped me to catch a glimpse of what it means that God should share our human life. It is part of a scene from *The Possessed* by Dostoyevsky (which I have re-translated and abridged) in which a son is born to Mary – Maria Shatova.

She has just returned after a long absence to the tumbledown shack of her husband Ivan in a squalid provincial town in Russia. She is expecting a child. It is not his, but he takes her in and fetches the midwife, Mrs Virginsky.

Daybreak was raw and cold. Ivan stood on the landing, just where he had stood when the conspirators had come upstairs ... The moans that had been coming from the bedroom became horrible, animal cries, unbearable, impossible. He wanted to stop his ears but couldn't; and he fell on his knees saying: 'Mary – Mary, Mary', without knowing what he did. Then there was a new, different cry. He started and rose from his knees. It was a baby's cry, weak and discordant. He made the sign of the cross and rushed into the room. The midwife held in her hands a little, red, wrinkled creature that was crying and moving its tiny arms and legs. It was terrifyingly helpless and, like a speck of dust, was at the mercy of the first puff of wind.

Mary seemed unconscious at first, but she soon opened her eyes and looked at Ivan ...

'A boy? Is it a boy?' she asked in a voice weakened by pain.

'Yes, it is', said the midwife, wrapping him in a blanket. When she had finished and was about to lay him down between two pillows, she asked Ivan to hold him for a moment. Mary stole a glance at him. He understood at once – and brought the baby close to the bed to show him to his mother.

'He's – pretty', she whispered with a smile.

'Just look at him staring', the midwife laughed. 'What a funny face he has, this little man.'

'Rejoice ... Mrs Virginsky, it's a great joy ...' Ivan mumbled with an idiotically blissful expression on his face.

'Joy', the midwife said, chuckling ironically as she busied herself in clearing things up, working with great speed and efficiency.

'The mystery of the arrival of this new creature is great and unfathomable, Mrs Virginsky, and it's very sad that you don't appreciate it', he went on incoherently, dazed and elated … 'There were two and now suddenly there's a third – a new human being, a new spirit, entire, complete, not made by human hands; a new thought, a new love. It's awe inspiring. There is nothing greater than this in all the world.'

'The nonsense this man talks!' the midwife said. 'It's a simple development of a biological organism, and there's nothing mysterious about it at all. The way you put it every fly would be a mystery. I can tell you one thing – there are useless people who should never have been brought into this world. First change the world (I say) so that they can be useful and then breed them. This one for example – he'll have to go to the foundling hospital in a couple of days time.'

'He's not going anywhere so long as I'm here', Ivan said firmly, staring at the floor.

'Why? Are you adopting him then?'

'I don't have to. He's mine already.'

… After that, Mary wouldn't let him leave her side. He had to sit close by her, and although she couldn't talk much she kept looking at him with a blissful smile. It was as though she had been transformed into a little girl again. It was like a re-birth. Ivan cried like a child and kissed her hands saying all sorts of nonsense in a wild, inspired and entranced tone of voice … He spoke to her about his friends; about how they were going to live now and forever, world without end; about the existence of God; and about everyone being so good. In their enthusiasm they wanted to look again at the baby, so he picked him up.

'Mary', he said, holding the child in his arms, 'this is the end of the old nightmare, of disgrace, death and decay.'

And he went out, only to be murdered in an act of gratuitous cruelty.

The points which this passage helps me to notice about the birth of Jesus are these:

First, it was a real birth – for Mary it meant real blood and real sweat, real toil and real tears.

Secondly, it was birth into the real world we know – squalid, criminal and ill-housed; birth into a world of real people, not just like the murderous terrorists but also like Mrs Virginsky, good at her job, cheerful, brisk, efficient, no-nonsense, but also somehow lacking in depth, without reverence, incapable of grasping the mystery, the sheer mysteriousness of life, brutally frank and matter-of-fact, bruising other people's feelings when they are most vulnerable, treading on their dreams with half-understood pseudo-Darwinian reductionism about human life being merely biological when the psalmist teaches us that it is 'little lower than the angels' (or even 'little lower than God') (Psalm 8:5), and with wrongheaded, pseudo-Marxist social idealism: 'First change the world and then produce babies.' Well, God didn't change the world first. He became a baby first, accepted the world as it was, and then started to transform it from within.

Thirdly, this incident can help us to see the nativity from Joseph's point of view, to understand what it must have meant for him to take responsibility for a child which was not his and for an event over which he had no control; to give a baby and its mother a name and a home and a start in life. It meant not only accepting the present with love and the past with forgiveness, it meant accepting the future with hope and with a trust in God, which was indistinguishable from his old love of Mary and his new love of the child. The Son of God had no legal claim on Joseph, but Joseph responded to him with love and adopted him as his own son. Human beings have no legal claim on God; but he loves us in Christ and adopts us as his children. This is love, St John teaches us, not that we loved God, but that he loved us and sent his Son to be the Saviour of the world (1 John 4:14).

Fourthly, by entering into human life as a baby, the Word of God, 'not able to speak a word',[1] had to learn a human language from his mother; God's agent at creation, without whom nothing was made that was made, had to learn from Joseph how to make tables and chairs; and he whose nature and whose name is love had to learn to love, just as we do, from the love of earthly parents, their love for each other and their love of him. What he learnt is what any child may learn and the wise and powerful overlook, namely that the true nature of love is the true nature of God and the true nature of God is the true nature of love: 'There were two and now ... there's a third ... It's awe inspiring; there is nothing greater than this in all the world.'

Lastly, I am reminded what a great risk God took in becoming a baby for us and for our salvation: 'A little, red, wrinkled creature ... crying and moving its tiny arms and legs ... terrifyingly helpless and, like a speck of dust, was at the mercy of the first puff of wind.' Naked, homeless, a refugee, reckoned to be illegitimate, in imminent danger of death at the hands of cruel men, sharing the poverty and uncertainty of the life of humankind as millions know it and thus closer to human life, more – not less – truly human than many of us are, drawing his first breath, opening his lungs with that sudden intense racking pain across the chest which is the first experience any of us has of independent life outside the womb, outside paradise, east of Eden, real pain, real tears, real cries foreshadowing from the first the cross of Calvary – Christmas Day and Good Friday being, as John Donne said, but morning and evening of the same day.

The whole of life and death and of the story of our redemption is there already in the crib, and, because it is a man-child in the image of the immortal God who has been born into the world, there is also, right from the start, a hint of transfiguration and of uncreated light and of Easter and of resurrection to eternal life.

'Mary', he said, holding the child in his arms, 'this is the end of the old nightmare, of disgrace, death and decay.'

THE INCARNATION IN A PICTURE

I have used a scene from *The Possessed* by Dostoyevsky to illustrate the birth of a boy child to Mary; but I doubt if, in a year's time, you will remember the story or the characters in it. For they are insubstantial and not particularly memorable; it is difficult to know what they look like; they exist, not in themselves, but in order to present ideas and hold conversations. In them words become flesh, just as in John's Gospel, where it is difficult to picture any of the characters, where at the beginning there is simply 'The Word' and at the end there is the promise of a quiet inward Spirit, breathed into the disciples on the evening of the first Easter day, to remain with them for ever.

How unlike Matthew and especially Luke. They write not like Dostoyevsky but like Tolstoy, with solid creatures of flesh and blood treading the earth, eating and drinking, interacting, doing deeds, depicted in deep glowing colours and surrounded by angels and innkeepers, shepherds and kings, men at arms, oxen and asses, beasts of the field and the whole company of heaven. And at the end, as in a melodrama, we wait for the Spirit who, when he does come at Pentecost, arrives in flames of fire with a sound like a rushing mighty wind, shaking the house and filling it with smoke, with stupendous audiovisual effects and a star-studded international cast of thousands (Acts 2:1–13).

I make this contrast, first because it really is there in the Bible. Secondly, because it is a sign of God's love for humankind that, when he chose to come in person into the world he had made, to save it from itself, he took a form which lent itself to different modes of expression, corresponding to the different types of person who would hear the message and bear it.

Let me illustrate that rather abstract point from the Gospels themselves. God spoke to the wise men from the East through a star because they were Gentiles and could only be approached indirectly through signs belonging to their own culture, which was steeped in astronomy and astrology. But he could speak directly in the words of an angel to the shepherds in the fields, as he had done to Mary in her home in Nazareth, because they were Jews and would know at least to some extent what he was talking about. So nowadays at Christmas time he speaks to some through tinsel and holly, through presents and good cheer, while to others he speaks through hymns and carols and the words of the Bible. But however varied the medium, at the heart of the message is Jesus Christ, true God and true Man, a babe born in Bethlehem, as it says at the beginning of the letter to the Hebrews, 'Long ago God spoke to our ancestors in many and various ways by the prophets, but in these last days he has spoken to us by a Son' (Hebrews 1:1–2a). The common factor in all these varied presentations of the truth is Jesus Christ, a babe born in Bethlehem.

Now, in addition to the novel, I want to share with you something of the painting which for me best conveys the meaning of that birth, that incarnation which is not just a mixture of human and divine, partly one thing and partly another, but a union which is wholly human and wholly divine at the same time. It is Rembrandt's *Holy Family with Angels* of 1645. It can be seen in the Hermitage in St Petersburg; and it is reproduced, with permission, on the cover of this book.

A generation after his great countryman Rubens had presented the Christian faith in splendid, triumphant and theatrical canvasses, Rembrandt turned away from the heroic and spectacular in order to concentrate instead on ordinary everyday life, on indoor domestic scenes and on the attempt to go beyond outward appearance to the expression of inner meaning. So his Holy Family is contemporary, not at all grand, dressed in ordinary clothes, living in a modest artisan dwelling where the living room is also the workshop. Mary, a Dutch peasant girl, is seated in the foreground, holding a book (presumably the Hebrew Scriptures) on her knee in her left hand while rocking or steadying with her right hand a Moses basket cradle which stands on two transverse wooden rockers on a plain deal floor. There is nothing out of the ordinary here, except that the shadows cast by the cradle indicate that a little light is coming from the child with his barely perceptible halo, tiny fingers and placid old man's face.

Joseph stands behind Mary shaping a yoke with a hand axe, the other tools of his trade hanging beside him on the wall. There is just a hint that when the grown Jesus says, 'My yoke is easy' (Matthew 11:30), he will be speaking with the proper pride of a craftsman from the little local firm of Joseph and Son, purveyors of fine, well-fitting yokes. As St John says in his Gospel, 'without him was not anything made that was made' (John 1:3 AV/KJV); and that applies equally to a small collection of wooden objects, now turned to dust, in Nazareth, as to the universe itself and the vastness of interstellar space.

The figure of Joseph is indistinct and scarcely finished. Some have criticised this, or sought to defend it by saying that originally it was much clearer, but the varnish has darkened and caused it almost to vanish. I think it is intentional. Joseph is as peripheral to Rembrandt as he was to the Gospel writers, sketched in to serve a purpose but not worked up into a full portrait. That comes later and is the work of the church, meditating for centuries on what it must have meant to be the adoptive father of the Son of God.

And it is true to life, naturalistic then as now, for the relationship between mother and child to form the focus of the scene.

So far everything in the picture has been ordinary, domestic, day-to-day Dutch interior. Only the top left-hand quarter is different. There angels are tumbling out of the darkness, conventional *putti* or little boy children like the holy child only with wings. This is Rembrandt's way of saying that this scene is absolutely ordinary and human but it is also absolutely extraordinary and divine. It is on earth and in time, but it is also in heaven and in eternity. We live in a real world in which fires burn and axes cut, in which children have to be wrapped up and looked after, in which ordinary everyday life is, well, ordinary everyday life. But it is also a world which is open to the skies, an earth which is interpenetrated by heaven and where angels come to us with messages of love, a world of imagination as well as of reason, a world of wonder and of awe.

There is something strange about the leading angel, coming in to land and so bracing himself with his arms held out horizontally and the wings more or less disappearing behind them. This little cherub is in the shape of a cross or rather in the attitude of the crucified. The child in the cradle has been born of an earthly mother like all of us, not only to live and work on earth like all of us but also to die like all of us. And then again, perhaps not quite like all of us. For his birth and life and work and death are not only ordinary, they are also extraordinary. They show God coming into the world he made out of love and to the humankind he made in his own image to take personal responsibility for the fact that the world is full of hatred and violence and the image is marred, disfigured, distorted and in some cases almost, but never quite, obliterated. If it had not been for that death and what happened after, we would never have known or cared about that birth and what happened after.

If it is through his crib that the carpenter's son comes to make things, then it is through his cross that he comes to mend them. And that, as they say, 'that costs'. So

> Like Mary let us ponder in our mind
> God's wondrous love in saving lost mankind.
> Trace we the babe who hath retrieved our loss
> From his poor manger to his bitter cross;
> Then may we hope, angelic hosts among
> To sing, redeemed, a glad triumphal song.[2]

THE MINISTRY OF JESUS
AS THE CROSSING OF BOUNDARIES[3]

The Palestine into which Jesus was born and where he exercised his ministry was full of borders: administrative, jurisdictional, linguistic, ethnic and religious, as well as geographical, bounded as it was and is by the Mediterranean to the west, the Jordan Valley with Lake Gennesaret and the Dead Sea to the east, the mountains of Lebanon to the north and the desert of the Negev to the south. Provincial boundaries included those of Judea and Galilee, the scenes of most of the action. They were separated from each other by Samaria, which was so hostile that most Jews preferred to take a long detour down from Jerusalem to Jericho, across the Jordan through Perea, then through the Decapolis, which as its name suggests was largely colonized by Greek speakers, and on to Galilee, which was itself bordered by pagan Syro-Phoenicia and Ituraea (subdivided into Ituraea, Trachonitis and Gaulanitis) and adjoining Abilene and Syria.

I say this, not as rigmarole, but simply to show how complex the situation was, rather like the states of former Yugoslavia today. Luke had to begin the third chapter of his Gospel by pointing out,

'In the fifteenth year of the reign of Emperor Tiberius, when Pontius Pilate was governor of Judea, and Herod was ruler of Galilee, and his brother Philip ruler of the region of Ituraea and Trachonitis, and Lysanias ruler of Abilene.' At their trials both Jesus and St Paul kept on being transferred from one local jurisdiction to another; and the Jewish religious authorities had a certain limited jurisdiction of their own, too, with the right to levy taxes in the outer court of the temple and to administer punishments, though not the death penalty by decapitation or crucifixion.

Moreover, the Jewish religion was characterized by the concept of separation. In the beginning, God, who unlike the gods of the heathen is separate from the world, creates by separation, light from darkness, night from day, and the sea from the dry land. He calls into being his people, the Jews, who are to be separate from the Gentiles. They adopt laws which insist, for example, on the separation of clean from unclean animals, of meat from milk, of linen from wool. They separate the Sabbath from the other days of the week. They emphasize the distinction between male and female in dress, tasks and behaviour.

Since the return from exile in Babylon there is a new, especially bitter form of division, namely between Jew and Samaritan. 'Jews do not share things in common with Samaritans' (John 4:9). By the time of Jesus they had adopted, though it ran counter to their own best insights, the distinction between slave and free. And Herod had rebuilt the temple as the architectural embodiment of the principle of division with a wall of separation between the Court of the Gentiles and the temple area proper, separate courts for men and women, an altar area for the priests, and the Holy of Holies for the high priest alone to enter on one special day of the year, Yom Kippur.

Now Jesus crosses every one of these lines, whether geographical, jurisdictional, legal, political, personal, ethnic, customary or taboo. We might even say that crossing boundaries is his typical activity. We have already followed his example, in our quest to penetrate the mystery of the incarnation, by crossing the boundaries between theology, fine art and literature. Nothing could be further from the spirit of Jesus than the rigid compartmentalisation of ideas, of artistic genres and especially of human beings, which characterised the ancient world (see chapter 6) and which still needs combating today. Is it a sign that God has a Jewish sense of humour, that he who taught us to pray 'forgive us our trespasses' should be the greatest trespasser of all, ignoring all man-made 'Keep Out' signs, and 'breaking every barrier down'?[4]

He begins his life on earth with a birth, which appears to transgress the bounds of decency and legitimacy, biology and possibility. The first events are the flight into Egypt and the return to Palestine, identifying him forever with those who are forced into exile against their own will, refugees and asylum seekers, the involuntary boundary crossers of our age. But that is just the overture.

The opera itself begins with him cleansing a leper; and the Evangelist emphasises that he 'stretched out his hand and touched him' (Mark 1:41), thus breaking a strict taboo and, indeed, a sensible hygienic precaution. (For the ministry of Jesus, I am basically following Mark's account.) In the most dramatic of all the healing stories, when the friends of a paralysed man break up the roof to let him down, Jesus not only heals him, but also scandalises the scribes by claiming that the Son of Man has power on earth to forgive sins (Mark 2:10). That is fighting talk. Judaism has a strong concept of forgiveness. It practically invented it; but, for the scribes, forgiveness belonged to God alone in heaven, and it would be experienced at the end of time at the last judgement. Jesus brings forgiveness out of the there and then into the here and now; and he not only exercises it himself, he also entrusts the task of forgiveness to his followers.

As if that is not enough, the next thing he does is to call Levi, a notorious tax gatherer, to follow him; and he joins him at table with 'many tax collectors and sinners' (Mark 2:15). We ought not to romanticise 'publicans', as the old versions call them. They were brutal and unscrupulous mafiosi, traitors and collaborators, the lowest of the low. We knew them well in what we used to call 'Communist-dominated lands'. But Jesus says of them, 'I have come to call not the righteous but sinners' (Mark 2:17). He then breaks the rules of fasting and compounds his offence by allowing and encouraging his disciples to break the Sabbath by plucking ears of corn. That may seem trivial and minimal; but a comparable act in the twentieth century, namely Mahatma Ghandi taking a pinch of salt from the sea, led to the overthrow of the British Empire in India. And Jesus claims, 'The Son of Man is lord even of the sabbath' (Mark 2:28). That is another boundary crossed.

He goes on to break the biggest taboo of all, destroying the absolutist claims to loyalty of the Near Eastern family group, by stating that anyone who does God's will is his brother and sister and mother (Mark 3:35). (Note that he is not encouraging us to be cavalier or libertarian; it is in order to do God's will, not just to please ourselves, that the tentacles of that dear octopus[5], the family, are to be cut.)

So far, Jesus has been teaching and healing in Galilee among his own people, the Jews. Now he leaves that and sets out with his disciples to cross Lake Gennesaret, the Sea of Galilee. This is the calculated crossing of a significant dividing line, for the lake was not an internal fishing pond; it was a frontier, a boundary between Jewish Galilee on the west and pagan territory to the east. With his word, 'Let us go across to the other side' (Mark 4:35), Jesus is deliberately leaving the known, the safe and the familiar, for the unknown, the alien and the dangerous. The voyage takes them through two storms. The first is a storm of wind and waves, which he calms with his word of command, 'Peace! Be still!' provoking the agonised question of the disciples, 'Who then is this, that even the wind and the sea obey him?' The second is a storm in a human heart, in the shattered personality of the Gerasene madman, a foreign maniac in pagan territory under Roman control.

We in the twenty-first century might well think that the power to quell a storm is more miraculous than the ability to heal even so serious a case of disintegrated personality. But is it? The most rebellious part of creation is not inanimate nature, not the weather, not even the tsunami of 2005 and Hurricane Katrina. It is the hearts and minds of men and women; and it required of Jesus more courage, more obedience to the Father's will, more divine energy to face his fellow human beings and subdue them, than it did to outface the storm. After all, it was not the wind or the waves which crucified Jesus; it was men and women, tossed about by our own disordered instincts and emotions and corporate insanities. It is not the weather which confronts us now with our most intractable problems; it is ourselves, our souls and bodies, which cry out for calming and correction and the healing touch of Christ.

'Who then is this?' If, as Mark intends, we take the two miracles together, we cannot fail to note that Jesus is portrayed as having power both over the turbulence of the sea and also over the fury of the Gentiles, a power which in Psalm 65:7 is ascribed to God alone, who 'stilleth the noise of the seas, and the noise of their waves, and the madness of the people'. No wonder that the disciples and the people of the land are terrified, the pagans even begging him to 'leave their neighbourhood' (Mark 5:17). Boundaries are dangerous places for all concerned; but they are also places where miracles can and do occur.

If the Jews were concerned about skin disease, they were even more concerned about blood, especially menstrual blood. They had elaborate rules both for avoiding it and also for periods of ritual uncleanness, which involved separation from the society of their fellow human beings, who would otherwise be defiled by contact with it. Jesus, having crossed back to the other side of the lake and on his way to heal Jairus's daughter, meets the need of the woman, who had been hemorrhaging for twelve years, with physical contact and his word, 'Daughter, your faith has made you well; go in peace, and be healed of your disease' (Mark 5:34).

I will not say much about his teaching, except on defilement, which is pertinent to this theme. For him, defilement is not an external matter, but an internal one. It is not what you touch or what you eat; it is what comes out of your heart and mouth, which defiles you. This is an astonishing reversal, revolutionizing morality, social customs and even dietary rules, the true reading of Mark 7:19 being, 'Thus he declared all foods clean.' It is all the more remarkable, when we consider how the mere presence of pigs is used in the story of the Gerasene demoniac, as in the parable of the Prodigal Son, to heighten the sense of strangeness and alienation, of being out of bounds.

One particularly pertinent anecdote begins with Jesus crossing the border of Tyre and Sidon and engaging in conversation, badinage even, with a woman whose daughter he heals. She is out of bounds fourfold to a young Jewish rabbi: female by gender, Canaanite by race, Syrophoenician by nationality and Greek by speech and culture. She combines an earthy sensuality with sophisticated decadence, a feisty, unattached woman who causes a scandal by taking the initiative and approaching him in public (Mark 7:24–30). But that doesn't inhibit Jesus or his healing power, any more than do the circumstances in which he meets a notoriously sinful Samaritan woman at Jacob's well (John 4:5–30).

John begins this section of his Gospel with the words, Jesus 'had to go through Samaria' (John 4:4), that is to say, he had an inner compulsion not to take the long way round beyond Jordan, but deliberately to cross frontiers and encounter the hated and despised aliens. Except, of course, that it was he, a Galilean Jew of the house of David, who was an alien among the Samaritans, descended as they were from *am ha'aretz*, the people of the land.

Of all the various groups of people whom Jesus ought to have avoided, the Samaritans were chief. Yet St Luke delights in telling the story of the grateful Samaritan (Luke 17:11–19); and in the tale of the Good Samaritan he records the most memorable of all Jesus' parables in phrases which have become part of our language (Luke 10:25–37).

One more example, among many possible ones. When, according to St John, Jesus at the Last Supper takes a towel, girds himself and washes the feet of his disciples (John 13:1–15), he is quite consciously doing work which was reserved for women, slaves and Gentiles, crossing over to them, identifying himself with these separated fellow human beings, subjected as it were to primitive forms of apartheid. No wonder St Paul was later to sum up the gospel in the words, 'no longer Jew or Greek ... slave or free ... male and female; for all of you are one in Christ Jesus' (Galatians 3:28).

Now all these examples have been taken from the life of Jesus Christ on earth. If we turn to Christian doctrine, we find, not surprisingly, that the same metaphor of boundary crossing applies. First, in creation, of which the Word is the agent ('without him not one thing came into being', John 1:3), he crosses the great divide between 'being' and 'non-being'. 'To be or not to be' was a question for him long before it was a question for Hamlet. Then in the incarnation he crosses the divide between the human and the divine, which is no problem for Graeco-Roman mythology, but is an insuperable barrier for Judaism and Islam. Next, through his cross and resurrection, he overcomes the fundamental division between life and death; he crosses the Jordan in both directions; he comes back from 'that undiscovered country from whose bourn no traveller returns'.[6] He has already transgressed a boundary and a taboo about death by touching the bier upon which lay the corpse of the widow's son at Nain (Luke 7:11–17).

In his letter to the Ephesians, St Paul sums up the extraordinary influx of the Gentiles and the expansion into Asia Minor, Greece and Italy of what had been a basically Jewish church confined to Jerusalem, with the striking phrase, 'He ... has broken down the dividing wall, that is, the hostility between us ... that he might create in himself one new humanity in place of the two, thus making peace, and might reconcile both groups to God in one body through the cross' (Ephesians 2:14–16). Of course, Paul is alluding to the inner temple wall; but none of us can now hear these words without recalling with gratitude to God the great events of 1989–90, of which the breaking down of the Berlin Wall was the most vivid and potent symbol.

Finally, St Paul, in that same letter to the Ephesians, encourages us to look forward to the end of the age, when all barriers, boundaries and divisions will have been overcome, when the Son will give everything back to the Father, and he will be all in all, 'according to his good pleasure that he set forth in Christ, as a plan for the fullness of time, to gather up all things in him, things in heaven and things on earth' (Ephesians 1:9–10). That will be the final frontier. Our faith and our hope are that Jesus Christ will cross that, too, and take us with him across the finite fences of space and time to enjoy peace at the last.

QUESTIONS

1. (a) How do artists, musicians and writers help us to understand biblical stories?

   (b) Give your favourite examples.

2. Should we 'first change the world and then produce babies'?

3. 'Beneath the angel strain have rolled two thousand years of wrong.' Is the incarnation the 'end of the old nightmare' or only 'the beginning of the end'?

4. 'If it had not been for (Christ's) death and what happened after, we would never have known or cared about (his) birth and what happened after.' Is that so?

5. In what ways is the crossing of boundaries characteristic of the ministry of Jesus?

CHAPTER 3

A Tree Falls in Siberia

Trials and Tribulations 1: The First Circle and Cancer Ward

The phrase 'if a tree falls in Siberia' goes back to Bishop George Berkeley (1685–1753). He claimed that 'to be is to be perceived' and that even if a tree fell unperceived in Siberia, it still existed and, indeed, fell, because it was continuously perceived by God.

Ever since I first went to the then Soviet Occupation Zone of East Germany in 1956, until the Berlin Wall fell in 1989, I worked closely with Christians 'behind the Iron Curtain', as we used to say. We in the West knew something of their sufferings, and we also knew that there was far more that we did not know. 'If a tree falls in Siberia' became part of my prayers. It assured me that when human beings fell in Siberia, as they did in their thousands, even millions, they and their sufferings were known to God. Eventually the victims found voices in the writings of Pasternak and Solzhenitsyn. Those voices resonate with the Passion narratives of the Gospels, which is not surprising, given the formative role of the Bible in Russian literature and of the Christian faith in Russian life.

Although he is the younger of the two, we listen first to the voice of Solzhenitsyn. Nothing illustrates better than his famous

Prayer the unique combination of tradition and originality in his writing:

> *How easy it is for me to live with You, Lord!*
> *How easy it is for me to believe in You!*
> *When my mind is distraught*
> *and my reason fails,*
> *when the cleverest do not see further*
> *than this evening and do not know*
> *what must be done tomorrow –*
> *You grant me the clear confidence*
> *that You exist and that You will take care*
> *that not all the ways of goodness are stopped.*
> *At the height of earthly fame I gaze*
> *with wonder at that path*
> *through hopelessness –*
> *to this point, from which even I have been able to convey*
> *to others some reflection of the light which comes from You.*
> *And You will enable me to go on doing*
> *as much as needs to be done.*
> *And in so far as I do not manage it –*
> *that means that You have allotted the task to others.*

Here Solzhenitsyn talks with God as with a friend. Such talk is unlike the dull sloganising of official Soviet literature. It is also unlike much conventional religious language; but it has the directness, crudity and disconcerting alternation between self-consciousness and self-forgetfulness of some of the psalms. Its hallmark is authenticity.

Solzhenitsyn uses living and lively language as an instrument for getting at the truth about himself and about the world. The author is thus both subject and object of a searching, probing vision, sustained by a passionate concern to understand the inner meaning of his own personal and social experience and clarified by the renunciation of despair, self-pity and false modesty. This true humility is characteristic of his heroes and heroines, all of whom are defeated, powerless and crippled by social, political and physical weakness, but ennobled by those qualities which in the Bible are ascribed to 'the poor'. The refusal to opt for comfortable words and the shortcuts of superficial optimism leads Solzhenitsyn through the experience and remembrance of anguish to that 'clear confidence' which enables him not just to stand his ground, but also to love life – ordinary, everyday life – and to *celebrate* it as no other contemporary writer. 'I absolutely do not understand why *Cancer Ward* is accused of being anti-humanitarian', he said to the Secretariat of the Writers' Union, 27 September 1967. 'On the contrary (in my novel) life conquers death, and the past is overcome by the future.'

Solzhenitsyn writes of resurrection with authority. He was born on 11 December 1918 – that is to say, after the Revolution. Unlike Pasternak, who was formed before 1917, Solzhenitsyn is 'Soviet Man', with as good a claim as any to have shared a typical fate. His father died a few months before his birth, and he was brought up by his mother through the hardships of the 1920s and 1930s, which are described in *Dr Zhivago*. In 1941 he graduated in physics and mathematics from Moscow University. He volunteered for the army and served a year in the ranks, was commissioned in the artillery, and was twice decorated for bravery.

Like many of his own characters, he fought right through the war in Russia, enduring unimaginable hardship, only to fall victim in 1945 not to the enemy, but to the charge of questioning in a private letter the strategical genius of Stalin – '*Usaty*', 'the man with the moustache', as he called him. He spent eight years in detention in a variety of camps – a general camp in the north, a construction camp, an institute for imprisoned scientists and a special political camp in Siberia, followed by exile 'in perpetuity'. He had survived the war. Now he survived the camps, only to face death a third time from inoperable cancer – and he survived again. He was released from exile after Khruschev's denunciation of Stalin at the Twentieth Party Congress in 1956.

A triple survivor, he came back from the *House of the Dead*, like Dostoyevsky a century earlier, to warn his brethren. The central experience of his life, to which reference is made in all his major work before *August 1914*,[1] is the period of detention; this is the central panel of a triptych: in the centre, Prison and Exile with the figures of Stalin and Beria; on the left War, with Hitler; on the right, Cancer, embodying Impersonal Evil. War, Prison, Exile and Cancer – these are the four plagues of Solzhenitsyn's Apocalypse; Hitler, Stalin, Beria and Impersonal Evil are the Horsemen (Revelation 6:1–8). His novels, which deal with this complex of experience, are the three best known and most widely available. They are closely related to each other and to the author's life.

THE FIRST CIRCLE

The most ambitious is also the least harrowing. *The First Circle*[2] was written painstakingly over a period of ten years, 1955–64. In it Solzhenitsyn draws upon his experience of the years 1945–49, from his arrest and incarceration until his transfer in a meat van to Karaganda in Kazakhstan.

The novel, for all its great length, covers only three days.[3] It is set in Mavrino, a special institute where prisoners who are also scientists are put to work inventing gadgets for the security forces. They have all come, like Solzhenitsyn, via the common camps for political and criminal prisoners north of the Arctic Circle and from construction camps in the Moscow region. Various experiences there are given in flash backs. This is typical of Solzhenitsyn's method, whereby he combines exceptional unity of time, theme and place (the last more or less guaranteed by a prison setting), with the disclosure of broad vistas of experience through the unlocking of memories.

Character after character is presented to us – sometimes one has the impression of reading a *Decameron*, or *Canterbury Tales*, as each man's story is interpolated. These are they who have come through great tribulation; all live with that particular past, knowing that it may well be their future too; and some of them are indeed transferred at the end, as Solzhenitsyn was, to a special camp for 'politicals', that is, a stricter regime than for criminals. All are victims of ludicrous denunciations and imaginary crimes such as intent to commit treason, failure to inform, escaping from German POW camps, slandering the security forces (*sic*), or simply possession of a flat or a wife coveted by a treacherous neighbour. They are victims of secret laws and abstract concepts such as the infamous Section 58 of the Penal Code. They are guilty only of existing, and punished because they are innocent. In this world turned upside down, where virtue is punished and vice rewarded, the Marquis de Sade's fantasies have come true.

When, in the words of Hannah Arendt, 'mankind [is] divided into those who believe in human omnipotence and those for whom powerlessness has become the major experience of their lives', the survivor is a sign of hope – but only if he survives not just biologically, not just as an animal but as a human being, with his moral and emotional faculties intact and purified. Solzhenitsyn's heroes, like their author, survive at great cost to themselves, not at the cost of others. Beaten to their knees, they can still say 'We did not bow down to idols; we did not collaborate with our oppressors; we did not betray our fellow men.' The heroes, like their author, have the unchallengeable authority of actual experience. This is the firm rock in that quicksand among literary forms, the autobiographical novel.

Providentially Solzhenitsyn, who has had Dostoyevsky's experience of prison and exile, has Tolstoy's literary gifts – the ability to observe and represent the surface details, the minutiae of routine, the setting of characters in society, the relationship between man and milieu. When he departs from what he has himself seen and observed, he nods. The description of Stalin as an old man is moving and credible, because Solzhenitsyn knows old men. He is not at his best when he tries to take us inside the mind of Stalin, for Stalin is for him what Napoleon was for Tolstoy – the incarnation of everything he disapproved of. In *The First Circle* he conveys the comedy of evil but not to the same extent the tragedy or the mystery. His Stalin is comparable with Adolf Hinkel in *The Great Dictator*, rather than with Stavrogin in *The Devils* or with Macbeth. It is great imaginative writers like Dostoyevsky and Shakespeare who can recreate from introspection the truth that is stranger than either fiction or history.

Yet simply to suggest these comparisons is only one step lower than the highest praise. Solzhenitsyn, like them, is a tragic comedian with a broad human sense of fun and of the ludicrous, set within the pitilessly clear-eyed quest for truth. In the West it is widely believed that Solzhenitsyn is primarily a protagonist of individual freedom, but this is to mistake a secondary effect for the main thrust. His overriding concern is for the truth, and for the truth in its full biblical range of meaning. Truth for him is not just factual accuracy, although that remains important. It means also trustworthiness, reliability and straightforwardness, as does the word *pravda* in Russian. Such is the truth, which makes free (John 8:32). Because he is writing in and about a society which is both given to the cult of the idols of the marketplace and also requires an exceptional degree of conformity and imposes exceptional constraints, the discovery of truth necessarily discloses the extent to which men are not free. Warders and *apparatchiki* are, if anything, less free than prisoners and patients. All are victims, but not all are innocent victims. Some are more guilty than others.

One of the most notable characteristics of Solzhenitsyn's novels is a strong element of judgement together with a high doctrine of human responsibility. They are not value free. They are vertebrate works of art in which the backbone is an implied and accepted scale of moral values, none of which is a novelty. Solzhenitsyn is a conventional moralist – and thus a comedian like Molière – in the sense that he reaffirms those things which people at all times and in all places have generally agreed to be right. False witness gets the shortest shrift at his hands, but coveting, idolatry and adultery are also reckoned to militate against truth and freedom.

If it was a shock for some of Solzhenitsyn's Soviet colleagues to be told that 'there are depths to which a writer will not sink,'[4] it must also be a shock for many of his Western literary contemporaries to see so strong a case made out for chastity and fidelity in *The First Circle*. In both cases the shock is a shock of recognition; we have been here before in the company of Tolstoy and Dostoyevsky. 'Like his predecessors, Solzhenitsyn plunges into the depths of man's consciousness, where neither capitalism nor communism nor The Great Society exists. And from this point of view his works, at the present moment, are of utmost significance for the Western world as well as to the Russian, from where they have come.'[5]

In contrast to the façades, the emptiness, the practised deceit and moral bankruptcy of the authorities, the prisoners come to the truth by rediscovering conscience as a human faculty. Their ordeal is a purgatory which leads them to the attainment of a fundamental moral vision, the knowledge of good and evil. As one of them, Nerzhin, says, 'Formerly I had no idea what good and evil were, and whatever was allowed seemed fine to me ... But the longer I sink into this inhumanly cruel world, the more I respond to those who ... speak to my conscience.' For this kind of prisoner social and physical descent is moral and spiritual ascent.[6] He is stripped to his essential self – a pure, purged self with nothing and no needs beyond the need to live. His poverty is great riches, his weakness the source of immense strength. Another prisoner, Bobynin, says to Abakumov,[7] 'You made a mistake there, chief. You have taken everything away from me. A man from whom you have taken everything is no longer in your power. He is free all over again.'

So it can be said of those who are shipped off as meat to Karaganda that 'there was peace in their hearts ... they were filled with the fearlessness of those who have lost everything – the fearlessness which is not easy to acquire, but which endures'. It was in prison that St Paul found the classic phrase for this experience, 'the peace of God, which surpasses all understanding' (Philippians 4:7). Solzhenitsyn's prisoners, remembering an earlier conversation about Dante's *Inferno*, wave goodbye to Mavrino with the words, 'That's not hell. Mavrino is the best, the highest, the *First Circle*. It is almost paradise.'

CANCER WARD

On Solzhenitsyn's release from prison camp in February 1953, he was condemned to exile 'in perpetuity' – not just *zhiznennaya ssylka* ('exile for life'), which had been the severest penalty in Tsarist Russia, but *navechno* ('eternally'), as Kostoglotov (the semi-autobiographical hero of the novel) keeps repeating. He settled in Kosh-Terek in southern Kazakhstan (the Uzh-Terek of the book), fell ill with cancer, and in 1955 travelled to Tashkent for treatment.

This is the time and place of the novel, set in a hospital in Uzbekistan on the eve of de-Stalinization.

Solzhenitsyn excels in depicting the routine of a closed institution,[8] the rituals of treatment, the effects of pain and of the proximity of death. Cancer, a greater leveller than socialism, has brought a cross section of stratified Soviet society together in one room. In the *Cancer Ward* (as in Chekhov's *Ward 6*[9]) there is scope and opportunity for great Russian conversations on literature, on ethics, on socialism and on the meaning of life. There is need, too, and the patients take up Tolstoy's insistent question 'What do men live by?' Some of them agree with his answer – Love. This is not a political or ideological answer, but a religious one.

Beyond the conversations and the analyses, there is something more, to which we can only give the name 'celebration'. *Cancer Ward* is a celebration of life – life in the face of death, life from the dead. It is for this reason that so much of the novel is taken up with Kostoglotov's problem about his treatment. The X-rays and hormones, which are to cure his stomach cancer, may affect his virility, and the question arises, 'Isn't the price too high?' This question vexes the minds of those who contemplate the cost of revolution. In conversation with the stricken Party member Rusanov, Kostoglotov says, 'There is nothing on earth for which I would pay *any* price'; and Solzhenitsyn's view appears to be that the means chosen in Stalinism kill those very qualities of truth, compassion, trust and care for neighbour without which the end of Communism cannot be realized.

Sologdin in *The First Circle* had said, 'Remember this: the higher the end the higher the means must also be! Unworthy means destroy the end itself.' A hundred years earlier, Ivan Karamazov, wrestling with his own despair, had argued that it is wrong to buy universal harmony at the price of even one suffering child.

Solzhenitsyn takes this classical argument against God and uses it against Stalin.

But not only against Stalin. Just as Chekhov's *Ward 6* was read as an allegory of Tsarist Russia, so *Cancer Ward* can be read as an allegory of the contemporary Soviet Union. It is doubtful whether it should be, for the allegorical method of interpretation lends itself too easily to simplistic exegesis at the political level. *Cancer Ward* is then reduced to what it has been accused of being, namely a snowball in the Cold War. And that is to trivialize.

It is more helpful to set Solzhenitsyn's novels within the tradition of nineteenth-century Russian poetic realism. By taking the actual, the local and the contemporary for what they were, and treating them with great seriousness, the Russian novelists were able to use 'reality' poetically or symbolically, and thus to disclose for people of other ages and other lands universal truths which speak to their condition also. As Solzhenitsyn said in an interview with the Czech journalist Pavel Licko about his controversial play *Candle in the Wind*, 'I wanted to point out the moral problems of society in technically developed countries, irrespective of whether they are capitalist or socialist.'[10] He is concerned with the general spiritual and moral crisis of the age, and with specific ideologies, policies and political systems only in so far as they get in the way of the truth and the fullness of human life.

Eventually Kostoglotov, too, chooses life, risking both the argument and also part of himself in order to save 'the main thing', reckoning that it is better to enter into life lame than to perish (Mark 9:45). At the end of the novel he is released from hospital, which has been the place of his wrestling with death, doubt and despair. Like Jacob at Peniel (Genesis 32:30–32), he passes on limping into the city, where he experiences everything – food, drink, the sight of animals, the feel of human beings, as on 'the first day of Creation'.[11] He delights in an apricot tree in bloom;

eats shashlik and ice cream; goes to the zoo and admires the Nilgai antelope. Then in the evening he boards a train and sets out for 'eternal exile', laid out as if dead on the luggage rack. He ends up with nothing but a tiny extra bit of life, but as this is lived in freedom, it has the quality of eternity; it is a token and foretaste of life eternal.

The whole novel leads up to this one day in the life of Kostoglotov. It is an Old Testament day, shot through with the great themes of Creation, Fall (there is 'an evil man' in the Zoological Garden), Judgement and Hope. It can be read as the prolegomenon to *One Day in the Life of Ivan Denisovich*, in which a thousand years – the sum of the prison sentences – is distilled into one yesterday, and that yesterday is a carpenter's Calvary.

QUESTIONS

1. (a) How far can you make Solzhenitsyn's prayer
your own?

   (b) Compare its final paragraph with Ignatius
   Loyola's 'Teach me, good Lord, to serve thee as
   thou deservest', especially the phrase 'to toil and
   not to seek for rest'.

2. 'War, Prison, Exile and Cancer – these are the four
plagues of Solzhenitsyn's Apocalypse.' What has
the twenty-first century added?

3. 'The higher the end the higher the means must
also be! Unworthy means destroy the end itself.'
Give examples in church and state and, especially,
locally and personally.

4. 'You will know the truth and the truth will make
you free' (John 8:32). What is the connection
between truth and freedom?

CHAPTER 4

A Tree Falls in Siberia

Trials and Tribulations 2:
One Day in the Life of Ivan Denisovich

In the late 1950s Solzhenitsyn put aside *The First Circle* for a while to write his masterpiece – a novella less than one-fifth the size of the novels. Published in 1962 as the first truthful account of life in the camps, *One Day in the Life of Ivan Denisovich*[1] was not only a political sensation, breaking a taboo, but also a literary landmark, for he achieves here a rare and perfect unity of form and content. The story is neither pure fiction, nor even the fictionalised autobiography of *The First Circle* and *Cancer Ward*. We are made scarcely aware of the narrator and totally unaware of the author, as everything is experienced and expressed by one simple 'little man', Shukhov.

The tale is told in his own words – but in the third person singular ('he'), not the first person singular ('I'). For this is how Shukhov experiences his own existence in the camp – as a subjected object and as an objectified subject. This device gives Solzhenitsyn the distance, the standing back from the picture, which is so important in coming to terms with painful, humiliating and embittering experience. The emotion is recollected, intensely recollected, but in tranquility. As Shukhov says of one of the other characters, 'he continued his story without self-pity, as if he were talking about somebody else.'[2] This is the quality which gives to Solzhenitsyn's anonymous victims their Homeric character.

> Shukhov finished up his gruel without making any effort to see who was sitting around him ... All the same, he noticed that when the man directly opposite him vacated his place, a tall, old man – U-81 – sat himself down ...
>
> Shukhov had been told that this old man had spent countless years in camps and prisons, and had never benefited from a single amnesty, and that whenever one ten year sentence ran out, then they slapped another one on him immediately. Now Shukhov examined him closely. Among all those men in the camp with bent backs, his back stood out as straight as a board, and it seemed as if he had put something on the bench beneath him to lift himself up ... The old man's eyes didn't dart around to see what was going on in the mess-hall, but were fixed above Shukhov's head at some invisible spot of his own. He ate the thin gruel with a worn wooden spoon at his own pace, but he didn't bend his head towards the spoon – but carried the spoon all the way to his mouth ... His face was quite drained of life, but did not look weak or unhealthy – rather, looked dark and as if hewn out of stone. And from his hands, which were big and cracked and blackened, you could see that not much soft work had come his way in all those years. But it was clear that the one thing he wasn't going to do was give in: he wasn't going to put his bread, like everybody else, straight down on the filthy table – but on a piece of cloth which had obviously been washed many times.[3]

In this vignette Solzhenitsyn (artist rather than propagandist) draws an individual human being out of darkness for a moment and then lets him slip back into obscurity. He sets him before the eyes of Ivan Denisovich and thus of the reader as a man who remains human in, and in spite of, his environment. U-81 has been tested, but through his testing he has preserved certain characteristics.

First, he is upright. In spite of everything he is not bent like a beast of the field; he retains this essential element of being made in the image of God.

Secondly, 'the old man's eyes didn't dart around to see what was going on in the mess-hall, but were fixed above Shukhov's head at some invisible spot of his own.' He is different, in that he lifts up his eyes and sees as one seeing the invisible (cp. Hebrews 11:8 – 16, 27).

Thirdly, we should note the way he eats. He does not bend his head to the spoon, but he carries the spoon all the way to his mouth. That is to say, he eats as though he were giving himself Holy Communion according to the rites and ceremonies of the Orthodox Church.

And last, the symbol par excellence of endurance and difference is that instead of putting the bread straight down on the table, he takes out a little square of carefully washed cloth and places the bread upon it. I ask, who habitually takes bread and places it on a little square of cloth?

We do not know – and I do not think it matters – whether Solzhenitsyn means to say in his allusive way that U-81 is a priest or bishop. He may well be. We know that many such have spent long periods in the camps.[4] U-81 may be a layman. But whatever his canonical status, he is a man in the image of God, formed by a long liturgical tradition, surviving and reflecting as in a mirror the glory of a suffering servant.

When I first read this page of *One Day in the Life of Ivan Denisovich* I thought of the collect for the Transfiguration, 'Grant unto us thy servants, that in faith beholding the light of thy countenance, we may be strengthened to bear the cross and be changed into his likeness from glory to glory.' The transformation of human suffering in the light of faith in Christ is a common factor in the works of Solzhenitsyn. He is not just life affirming; his work is truly eucharistic, for in it 'life conquers death, and the past is overcome by the future'.

Solzhenitsyn was able to exhume an old, and comparatively rare, uniquely Russian literary form – the *skaz*, or tale, in which everything is seen through one pair of eyes and spoken by one pair of lips exclusively in the language of the milieu. Shukhov is a semi-literate carpenter, average man, not capable of discussing or even of understanding the moral and political implications of his situation. Like a sheep before its shearers he is a dumb beast – patiently suffering, but surviving and vindicated in his own style, which is a marvellous mixture of Russian colloquialisms, prisoners' slang, Soviet jargon and old soldiers' idioms and obscenities – crude, racy and alive – in contrast to the dull repetitiousness of official literature.

It is the very absence of intellectualisation, rationalisation, indignation and explanation which gives *One Day in the Life of Ivan Denisovich* something of the deadpan, take-it-or-leave-it plasticity of the Passion narrative in the Gospels, which are also written in a common non-literary language. It, too, allows and invites, but does not compel, response. A work of art like this is the polar opposite of argument, persuasion and propaganda; and it will outlive them all, because it shares in the given-ness of creation itself as well as in the suffering inherent in creativity.

Since the time of Mikhailovsky and Tolstoy, Russian intellectuals and students have tried to 'go to the people' – to get under the skin of the *moujik*, the collective farm worker or the proletarian. The prison camps have given Solzhenitsyn the opportunity to discover, what Dostoyevsky discovered in Siberia too, that real unity and identity with his fellow man as fellow sufferer, which escaped not only a squire like Tolstoy but even so notable a proponent of Socialist Realism as Sholokhov, whose Cossacks in *Quiet Flows the Don* are all made of cardboard – brightly painted, thick cardboard to be sure – but not flesh and blood. Solzhenitsyn adds insult to injury by excelling also in just those literary effects which Socialist Realism aspires in vain to achieve: in the depiction of the actual rhythms of work, of the dignity of labour, of joy in achievement and pleasure in the routine of a ward, a signal box or an office.

The 1960s were witnessing the decline of the proletarian novel, which had been the darling of the Party since the success of *Cement*[5] in 1925. For all the official exhortation and support, there is no example of even average merit. The best is one in which the authoress just fails to integrate the love life of the protagonists with her account of the gasification of brown coal. Yet here is how Shukhov finished his working day on the enforced construction of a power station in the freezing tundra, on an empty stomach, with inadequate equipment and organisation. This is the beginning of a passage, which is fifteen pages long – or one tenth of the whole novella:

> He worked well and swiftly, but his thoughts were not on his immediate work. His thoughts and his eyes were concentrated on the wall below the ice, the outside wall of the power station, two blocks thick. He didn't know the mason who had worked on that part of the wall before him, but he was either an idiot or an incompetent. Shukhov felt at one with the wall as if it were his own. There – there was a gap which it would be impossible to level out in one row; he'd have to do it in three, each time adding the mortar a little more thickly. And here the outer wall was swelling out – it would take two rows to straighten that. He divided up the

wall in his mind into the place where he'd lay blocks, from the left-hand corner, the stretch Senka was working on – on the right, and as far as where Kilgas was. There, on the corner on the right, he reckoned that Kilgas wouldn't hold back, would lay a few blocks for Senka to make things easier for him. And before they finished tinkering in the corner, Shukhov on his side would have more than half the wall up so that his pair did not fall behind. He made a note as to how many blocks he would have to lay where.[6]

And this is the end:

And as the gang-leader descended the ladder with resolute tread, Shukhov called after him, 'Why do the swine give us such a short working day? You've only got going on your work, and they knock you off!'

Shukhov was left with deaf Senka now. You didn't talk much with him, but you didn't need to: he was smarter than them all, he understood without words.

Slap on the mortar! Down with the block! Press down! Check! Mortar. Block. Mortar. Block...

The boss had said not to worry about the mortar – chuck it over the wall and push off. But Shukhov wasn't made that way, and eight years of camp life hadn't altered him: he still worried about every little thing and every piece of work – and he hated waste.

Mortar. Block. Mortar. Block...

'We've finished ...' Senka shouted. 'Let's be off!'

He seized a hod and went down the ladder.

But Shukhov – and the guards could have put the dogs on him now, it would have made no difference – ran back to have a look round. Not bad. He ran over and looked along the wall – to the left, to the right. His eye was true. Good and straight! His hands were still good. He ran down the ladder.[7]

Solzhenitsyn is master of that art which conveys the dynamics of morale, the way in which a man can get caught up in a task and a team, and surpass himself, even when it is not to his own immediate advantage. Ivan Denisovich's power station is a Russian *Bridge over the River Kwai*. There is a similar moment as his group races another to avoid being last in for roll call. It is felt and perceived with all the terror and intensity of a child running late to school in the days of corporal punishment. And his guards – the brutal kickers and pushers, thieves, torturers, scroungers and killers – common criminals set to oppress the politicals – these guards who all the day have been 'them', become for the duration of the race 'us', while the fellow prisoners in the other gang become temporary enemies – 'them'.

But not for long; 'Eight years as a convict had not turned [Shukhov] into a jackal.' He survives as a moral human being – though with the morality appropriate to the extreme situation. There the first law is 'Thou shalt survive', and the second is, 'but not at the expense of your fellow sufferer.' It is as right for Shukhov to scrounge a second bowl of gruel as it was for King David to eat the shewbread (Matthew 12:3–4; see 1 Samuel 21:1–6). Food and drink convey not just biological life – animal vitality – but also human well-being. Shukhov has learnt the value of the simple life, drawing sustenance from fleeting moments of achievement and bodily satisfaction. Bread and soup are for him the sacrament of life abundant:

> It was at this evening count, when they returned through
> the camp gates, that the prisoners felt most weather-beaten,
> cold and hungry – and their bowl of thin, hotted-up cabbage
> soup in the evening was, for them, like rain in a drought.

They swallowed it in one gulp. That bowl of soup was more precious to them than freedom, more precious than their previous life and the life which the future held for them ...[8]

Shukhov took off his cap and rested it on his knee ... He began to eat. First of all, he drank just the watery stuff at the top. As it went down, the warmth flooded through his whole body – and his insides seemed to be quivering in expectation of that gruel. Goo-ood! It was for this brief moment that a prisoner lived!

And now Shukhov had no complaints – about the length of his sentence, about the long day they had had, about the Sunday they would not be having. Now he thought: 'We'll survive! We'll get through it all! God grant that it'll end!'[9]

Thus sustained, Ivan Denisovich survives as his own unique self – enjoying himself in suffering imposed by man and nature.[10]

Solzhenitsyn is not the first author to take 'one day' as the subject of a book. Tolstoy had done this in his early essay in naturalism, *Twenty-Four Hours*, and James Joyce in *Ulysses* unfolds the famous 'Bloomsday'. But Solzhenitsyn invests it with unique significance. The day is important as such, both because it is a measurable fraction of prison sentences described in terms of the passage of time – five years, ten years, twenty-five years – and also because time is precious. Shukhov apprehends it as a gift, indistinguishable from the gift of life itself. For him in Karaganda, as for Kostoglotov in Tashkent, a day is no mere unit of chronological time. It is also time charged with eternity. This day, in a week in which 'the authorities have taken away Sunday again', is a holy day.

But how? Who hallows it? Not the authorities. Nothing indicates their cosmic impiety more than their pretension to control time. 'No clocks ticked here' (one of those marvellous details which become symbols through the transformation of the obvious into the significant): 'No clocks ticked here; the prisoners were not permitted to carry watches; the authorities told the time for them.'[11] Nor is the sanctification of time a function of the hero. Shukhov is average man, with a conventional Russian Orthodox background. He believes a bit, but not too much; and there are elements of superstition in his folk religion. We may smile at his simple belief, that God breaks up the moon monthly to replace fallen stars, but you need to be more credulous than that, Solzhenitsyn implies, to believe that Stalin invented radar and penicillin or that Bukharin was an enemy of the people. Shukhov stands between the official atheists on the one hand, and his mate, the pious Baptist Alyosha, on the other.

With Alyosha (who is clearly named for Dostoyevsky's Alyosha Karamazov), Solzhenitsyn broke another taboo. This is the first wholly sympathetic account of a believer in Soviet literature, and it is drawn from life. Alyosha takes upon himself the sacerdotal task of seeing to it that time is hallowed, and that the day in the life of Ivan Denisovich is given a structure. He reads his hidden Bible aloud morning and evening. We, with Shukhov, overhear him and participate – at a certain distance and with the slightly irritated sense of gratitude of villagers, hearing church bells calling to Morning and Evening Prayer. In the morning, Shukhov hears, 'But let none of you suffer as a murderer, a thief, a criminal, or even as a mischief maker. Yet if any of you suffers as a Christian, do not consider it a disgrace, but glorify God because you bear this name' (1 Peter 4:15 – 16). Solzhenitsyn is too great an artist, and he has too high a regard for the unglossed word of God, to add any comment.

Within the limits of this novella, which include, remember, the limits of the hero's intellect and imagination, there is no place for the far-ranging metaphysical explorations into faith and doubt in which Dostoyevsky excels – just a little conventional barrack-room banter.[12] In the evening Shukhov teases Alyosha about prayer; his own petitions come back marked 'rejected', and prayer didn't get Alyosha a lighter sentence (he had got his 25 years in fact for attending a prayer meeting in the Caucasus).

> 'But we didn't pray for that, Ivan Denisovich!' Alyosha persisted, and with the Gospels in his hands, he moved closer to Shukhov, right up to his face. 'Of all earthly and transitory things our Lord commanded that we should pray only for our daily bread ...'
>
> 'Our bread ration, you mean?' asked Shukhov. Alyosha went on exhorting more with his eyes than with his words, and he laid his hand on Shukhov's ...
>
> 'Why do you want freedom?' asked Alyosha. 'If you were free, the remnants of your faith would be overgrown with thorns! You should rejoice that you are in prison! Here you have time to think about your soul! Paul the Apostle said: "What mean ye to weep and to break mine heart? For I am ready not to be bound only, but also to die for the name of the Lord Jesus ..."' (Acts 21:13).[13]

Here we have all the strength as well as the limitations of a deeply interiorised pietism, which neither Shukhov nor Solzhenitsyn shares. They do not share it; they love life and freedom too much; but they do not despise it either. Indeed, the echoes of St Paul's 'I am ready to die' have been heard in an open letter by Solzhenitsyn to the Fourth Soviet Writers' Congress dated 16 May 1967, and we know from his other writings and his famous prayer that he is a deeply religious man, believing, and venerating the tradition of belief as a repository of obvious values in a topsy-turvy world. It seems that his dormant or latent Russian Orthodox faith was revivified in the camps by his encounter with Protestantism, with Baptists like Alyosha and with Baltic Lutherans, of whom he always writes with the utmost respect for their probity and piety.

Alyosha and Shukhov are interrupted by a shout: 'Recount!' Again, another roll call in the freezing cold; and so to bed, and to that miraculously understated final paragraph, where all the fruit of the Spirit (Galatians 5:22–23) is contained within pathetically narrow horizons, limited vocabulary and restricted sensibility. It is treasure in earthen vessels, a triumph of disciplined creativity and the summit of the twentieth-century novel:

> He hid his head in the thin, unwashed blanket, and … went off to sleep, completely content. Fate had been kind to him in many ways that day: he hadn't been put in the cells, the gang had not been sent to the Socialist Community Centre, he'd fiddled himself an extra bowl of porridge for dinner … he'd been happy building that wall … And he hadn't fallen ill…
>
> The day had gone by without a single cloud – almost a happy day.
>
> There were three thousand, six hundred and fifty three days like that in his sentence, from reveille to lights out.
>
> The three extra days were because of the leap years…[14]

QUESTIONS

1. 'Distance is ... important in coming to terms with painful, humiliating and embittering experience.' Is it?

2. 'It is as right for Shukhov to scrounge a second bowl of gruel as it was for King David to eat the shewbread.' Is it? If so, why?

3. Time is 'a gift indistinguishable from life itself'. How do we waste time? How do we hallow time?

4. In what ways can life conquer death, in camps and cancer wards today?

CHAPTER 5

The Vine

Jew and Gentile

We think of Boris Pasternak, not only as one of the outstanding literary figures of the twentieth century and of Russian literature, as the author of innumerable and incomparable poems, alas unavailable to us except in inadequate translations, but also as a heroic critic of Stalinist communism, unfairly deprived of a Nobel prize by the Soviet literary establishment for his uniquely lovely 'novel in prose' – *Doctor Zhivago*, first published in English in 1958. And yet David Ben-Gurion, the first Prime Minister of the newly created state of Israel, described that novel as 'one of the most despicable books about Jews ever to be written by anyone of Jewish origin'.[1] How can that be? How could so fine a spirit as Pasternak speak ill of the vine, which the Lord had brought out of Egypt at the Exodus (Psalm 80:8), and now, after many vicissitudes, replanted in Palestine?

In a long sprawling novel of over five hundred pages there are two passages, one near the beginning and one near the end, which touch upon the question of the Jews and the nations, plus a couple of references in the Lara poems, notably 'The Miracle' and 'Hamlet'. The only recognisably Jewish character in the book, Zhivago's lifelong friend Misha Gordon (Gordon in Russian being a Jewish, not a Scottish, name), is wholly likeable and positively presented. The reason must be that Ben-Gurion was a Zionist and Pasternak an assimilationist. It is easy for Christians to overlook the depth of animosity between those holding these two positions; and of course we now look back upon the first half of the twentieth century through the twin lenses of our knowledge of the Shoah, the Holocaust, and of the founding of the state of Israel and the moral ambiguities of its struggle to maintain itself in a hostile environment.

Pasternak, in his day and situation, was scarcely aware of the significance of these two epics. They were taboo subjects in the Soviet Union. Soviet propaganda played down the importance of Auschwitz and of the predominance of Jews among its victims, even though it had been liberated by the Red Army. Only in 1948 did the spontaneous enthusiasm of thousands of Soviet Jews for Golda Meir, the Foreign Minister of Israel, on a visit to Moscow arouse Stalin's suspicions, suspicions of the new state's possible influence on the morale and self-understanding of Soviet Jews. He mistrusted anything spontaneous; and the demonstrations led to a new injection of anti-Semitism into the normally indiscriminate political oppression of the day, to attacks on Jewish cultural figures and on Yiddish theatre and publications and, in 1952, on the 'rootless cosmopolitans' of the notorious so-called Doctor's Plot. These were not good times to be of Jewish origin in the Soviet Union.

Boris Pasternak had been born in Moscow, the historic capital of Tsarist Russia, in 1890, into a family which was Jewish on both sides. His mother, Rozaliya Isadorovna Kaufmann, was a distinguished concert pianist and music teacher, who gave up a glittering career to care for her family. His father, Leonid, was a gifted painter, a friend of Tolstoy and, eventually, Professor at the Moscow College of Painting, Sculpture and Architecture, under the patronage of the Imperial Court. He did not have to undergo the customary formality of outward conversion to Russian Orthodoxy, which indicates a certain metropolitan tolerance, or at least laxity, so conspicuously lacking for the overwhelming majority of the Tsar's Jewish subjects in the Pale of Settlement, which stretched through Lithuania, Poland, White Russia and the Ukraine, from the Baltic to the Black Sea, and where sporadic pogroms led to the great emigrations of the 1880s and 1890s to Western Europe and the United States.

Unusually, the Pasternaks were not Ashkenazy but were descended from a Sephardic family, which had settled in southern Russia in more tolerant times, when it needed colonists in the eighteenth century. The background of both Roza and Leonid was that of the cultured and cosmopolitan Jews of Odessa, even if they eventually settled in conservative, traditionalist, Orthodox and nationalist Moscow. Boris became from birth a citizen of the whole wide world of music and the arts, of philosophy and literature. It is not surprising that he reacted so strongly against the stifling conformity and chauvinistic nationalism of atheistic Communism in its Stalinist form, which he came to regard as a great leap backwards into the world BC, the ancient world before the coming of Christ. What is surprising, and indeed disconcerting, is that he did not always distinguish sufficiently clearly between the worlds of Graeco-Roman paganism on the one hand and of the Hebrew Scriptures on the other, using both rather indiscriminately as metaphors for contemporary Communism.

His rich cultural heritage did not, however, include the faith of his fathers. Leonid and Roza were, as was typical of their milieu, thoroughly secularised and integrated into Russian society. He was taken to be baptised at an early age, apparently without protest, by his Russian Orthodox nurse, Akulina Gavrilovna. Some doubt has been cast, not least by his sisters, on whether this semi-secret event ever took place at all. Pasternak was an exceptionally elusive person, who delighted in covering his tracks with mystery and obfuscation.

However, in later life Pasternak certainly regarded himself as a Christian, though, in accordance with his personal credo of individual freedom, as a decidedly non-conforming one. He spoke of Christianity as one of the principal inspirations of his poetry and of his novel, rejecting any dogmatic interpretation of them, but calling his faith 'the source of my originality'. Indeed, the two passages and the two poems in *Dr Zhivago*, to which Ben-Gurion objected, should be taken primarily as a positive portrayal of the difference which the coming of Christianity made to the world, rather than as a negative account of Judaism. But he was completely undogmatic and eclectic, picking, often with great intuitive insight, the aspects of Christianity which most appealed to him and seeing it as a repository of self-evidently humane and civilising values in comparison with the crude neobarbarism of Soviet society.

His great contemporary, the Petersburg poet Osip Mandelshtam, is less brilliant in his insights but consistently more profound in his appreciation both of his Jewish heritage and of Christian theology. 'Judaism', he notes in his memoirs, 'is like a grain of musk that will permeate the whole house.' But after his tragic death in prison camp his widow, Nadezhda, in her wonderful memoir *Hope against Hope*, comments that, by contrast with the poetess Anna Akhmatova, he 'was rather afraid of the Old Testament God and His awesome, totalitarian power. He used to say … that, with its doctrine of the Trinity, Christianity had overcome the undivided power of the Jewish God. Undivided power was for us, of course, something of which we were very afraid.'[2]

Pasternak would not, could not, have said that; but he does make a similar point in the second of the two passages, which

Ben-Gurion so disliked, in a more poetical, less theological way, with a long, rambling discourse by a minor and incidental character, Sima. She contrasts the Exodus, the crossing of the Red Sea by the people of Israel under the leadership of Moses, with the Annunciation of the birth of Christ to the Blessed Virgin Mary on the basis of a parallel, which is drawn in the liturgy, between these two events. She puts the Israelites together with the Egyptians and the Romans as typical of the ancient world, in which everything is public, powerful and political. It soon becomes clear that the author's target is not Judaism (or indeed ancient Egypt or ancient Rome) but contemporary Communism with its massive attack on private and personal life in the name of the collective and the nation. She says of the incarnation:

> From now on the basis of life is no longer to be compulsion, it is to be that very same inspiration – that's what the New Testament offers – the unusual instead of the commonplace, the festive instead of the workaday, inspiration instead of compulsion.
>
> You can see what an enormously significant change it is. Why should a private human event, completely unimportant if judged by ancient values, be compared to the migration of a whole people?
>
> Something in the world had changed. Rome was at an end. The reign of numbers was at an end. The duty, imposed by armed force, to live unanimously as a people, as a whole nation, was abolished. Leaders and nations belonged to the past. They were replaced by the doctrine of personality and freedom. The story of human life became the life-story of God and filled the universe. As it says in the liturgy for the feast of the Annunciation, Adam tried to be a God and failed, but God was made man so that Adam should be made God.[3]

In the circumstances of the Soviet Union it was of the utmost importance to Pasternak that God should deal directly with individuals, as well as with nations and humankind as a whole. He was particularly inspired by what he understood to be the relationship between Christ and Mary Magdalene. An explicit connection is made between her and Lara, the heroine of the novel, and two of the poems in the book are devoted to her. One passage, near the beginning of the book, I find particularly moving, not least because it sheds light on what worship means to me and, I believe, to many.

> Lara was not religious. She did not believe in ritual. But sometimes, to enable her to bear her life, she needed the accompaniment of an inward music and she could not always compose it for herself. That music was God's word of life and it was to weep over it that she went to church.
>
> Once ... she went to pray with such a heavy heart that she felt as if at any moment the earth might open at her feet and the vaulted ceiling of the church cave in. And it would serve her right ...
>
> In the time it took Lara ... to make her way past the worshippers ... buy two candles ... and turn back, [the deacon] had rattled off the nine Beatitudes at a pace suggesting that they were quite well enough known without his help.
>
> Blessed are the poor in spirit ... Blessed are they that mourn ... Blessed are they that hunger and thirst after righteousness.
>
> Lara shivered and stood still. This was for her. He was saying 'Happy are the downtrodden.' There is something to be said for them. They have everything before them. That was what he thought. That was Christ's opinion of it.[4]

This is the gospel for the teenage mistress of a middle-aged *roué*. It is the gospel of Christ.

To return to the main point, it cannot be stressed too strongly that Pasternak's critique of what he saw as Jewish nationalism was not anti-Semitic in the modern sense of the word. All forms of racism were equally abhorrent to him. Rather it was illustrative of his wider critique of nationalism, especially the Great Russian chauvinism of Stalinist Communism. Indeed, he expressed compassion for the sufferings of the Jews of Tsarist Russia. Earlier in the novel Zhivago rebukes a Cossack for humiliating an old Jew in front of his family. He says to his friend Gordon,

> 'It is terrible ... You can't imagine what this wretched Jewish population is going through in this war. The fighting just happens to be in their Pale of Settlement ... Why should they be patriotic when the enemy offers them equal rights and we do nothing but persecute them? ... There is something paradoxical at the very root of this hatred of them. It is stimulated by the very things which should arouse sympathy – their poverty, their overcrowding, their weakness and their inability to fight back. I can't understand it. There is something fateful about it.' Gordon did not reply.[5]

This incident leads into the other disputed passage, which begins with a contrast between the respective styles of nationalistic leadership of the Tsar and the Kaiser, again making it clear that the critique is a critique of nations and nationalism, in a word of the Gentiles, rather than of Israel, except in so far as Israel tried to be a nation like other nations. But Gordon takes up the theme, as Henry Gifford says in his excellent book on Pasternak, 'deploring segregation on the part of the Jews since they are destined above all peoples to transcend their racial identity and to be "dissolved without trace among the others whose religious foundations they have themselves laid."'

It is on this basis that Gordon (not Zhivago and doubly not Pasternak himself) criticises the Gentiles in general.[6] He then goes on to criticise the Jews in particular, quite exaggeratedly in my opinion:

> Their national idea has forced them, century after century, to be a people and nothing but a people – and the extraordinary thing is that they have been chained to this deadening task all through the centuries when all the rest of the world was being delivered from it by a new force which had come out of their own midst.

He continues, with compassion it is true but also with a certain one-sidedness:

> In whose interests is this voluntary martyrdom? Who stands to gain by keeping it going, so that all these innocent old men and women and children, all these clever, kind, humane, people should go on being mocked and slaughtered throughout the centuries.

He turns his indignation away from the persecutors onto the Zionists and says,

> Why don't the intellectual leaders of the Jewish people ever get beyond this facile Weltschmerz and irony? Why don't they – even if they have to burst like a boiler with the pressure of their duty – dismiss this army which is forever fighting and being massacred nobody knows for what? Why don't they say to them: 'That's enough. Stop now. Don't hold on to your identity, don't all get together in a crowd. Disperse. You are the first and best Christians in the world. You are the very thing against which you have been turned by the worst and weakest among you.'[7]

There is no reply to this tirade. The conversation and indeed the chapter end there; and no more is heard of this topic for nearly three hundred pages. It is as if the real-life Pasternak realises that in the fictional person of Gordon he really has gone too far, and steps back in alarm. No wonder Ben-Gurion took it personally and reacted accordingly; but it had not been directed at him. It was directed at Lenin and Stalin, of whom Zhivago was to say,

> Revolutions are made by fanatical men of action with one track minds, men who are narrow-minded to the point of genius. They overturn the old order in a few hours or days … but for decades thereafter, for centuries, the spirit of narrowness which led to the upheaval is worshipped as holy.[8]

It was the spirit of narrowness which Pasternak was combating throughout his entire life and work. For that reason alone we should concentrate, not on the few ill-judged negative words about the Jews in this passage in *Dr Zhivago*, but rather on the many positive words there about the effect and meaning of the incarnation, which is his chief concern. Gordon is speaking:

> What are all these nations we talk about anyway, now, in the Christian era? They aren't just nations – they are nations made up of individuals who have been converted, transformed. The point about them is their transformation, not their loyalty to their ancient ways.
>
> Now what do the Gospels say about it? To start with, the Gospels don't lay down a law – they aren't an assertion: 'It's like this and like that.' The Gospels are an offer, a naïve and diffident offer (or, an offer to the naïve and diffident): 'Would you like to live in a completely new way? Would you like to enjoy spiritual beatitude?' And everybody was delighted, they all accepted, they were carried away by it for thousands of years …

When the Gospels say that in the Kingdom of God there are neither Jews nor Gentiles, do they just mean that all are equal in the sight of God? I don't believe it means only that – that was known already – it was known to the Greek philosophers and the Roman moralists and the Hebrew prophets. What the Gospels tell us is that in this new way of life and of communion, which is born of the heart and which is called the Kingdom of God, there are no nations, but only persons.

Now you said that facts by themselves don't mean anything – not until meaning is put into them. Well, the meaning you have to put into the facts to make them relevant is just that; it's Christianity, it's the mystery of personality.[9]

And right at the start of the book, Zhivago's uncle the Tolstoyan priest Nikolay Nikolayevich (who is based to some extent on the composer Skriabin) says of the ancient world:

Rome was a flea market of borrowed gods and conquered peoples, a bargain basement on two tiers – earth and heaven – slaves on one, gods on the other. Dacians, Herulians, Scythians, Samaritans, Hyperboreans. Heavy, spokeless wheels, eyes sunk in fat, bestialism, double chins, illiterate emperors, fish fed on the flesh of learned slaves. Beastliness convoluted in a triple knot like guts. There were more people in the world than there have ever been since, all crammed into the passages of the Coliseum and all wretched.

And then, into this tasteless heap of gold and marble, He came, light-footed and clothed in light, with His marked humanity, His deliberate Galilean provincialism, and from that moment there were neither gods nor peoples, there was only man – man the carpenter, man the ploughman, man the shepherd with His flock of sheep at sunset, man ... who is sung in lullabies and portrayed in picture galleries the world over.[10]

'Neither gods nor peoples – only man.' This is the understanding of the coming of Christ into the world, which is expressed diffusely throughout *Dr Zhivago* and in concentrated form in the Lara poems. These are appended to it and they are the key to understanding it, notably the first, 'Hamlet', which contains the oft-quoted and much misunderstood line, 'I'm alone; all drowns in Pharisaism' (see chapter 7).

From this it is clear that when Pasternak uses the word 'Pharisaism', as he does here, he is not referring primarily to the historical party within Judaism, which played such a significant part in the New Testament and to which Jesus himself was much closer than has been traditionally assumed. 'Pharisaism' was for him a poetic code word for the Soviet literary establishment, as it was for his great contemporary, Anna Akhmatova, who described as 'his latest clash with "Pharisaism"' an incident involving Krivitsky, the deputy editor and power behind the throne of the influential literary journal *Novy Mir*.[11] Metaphors may give rise to misunderstanding, which is the risk they run in aiding understanding.

In 1969 I was in the Soviet Union on a delicate mission for the World Council of Churches to do with the schism between the congregations of the official Baptist Union and those of the dissidents or *initsiativniki*. We were, of course, under close surveillance throughout. On one occasion I took advantage of my privileged status as the holder of a British passport and exit visa to speak up for the claims and rights of individuals over against the collective; and to strengthen my point I quoted: 'I'm alone. All drowns in Pharisaism.' On more than one occasion later people came up to me and whispered conspiratorially, '*Ya odin, vsyo tonyet v phariseistve'*, that phrase having become a kind of badge or coded recognition sign for the like-minded.

Thirty years later, after the fall of Communism, I was greeted out loud at the Millennium celebrations of the Russian Orthodox Church in Moscow by a Baptist pastor, who recognised me, with the ringing declaration, '*Ya odin, vsyo tonyet v phariseistve* – I'm alone. All drowns in Pharisaism', thus demonstrating that nothing is more effective than poetry in making thoughts and sentiments memorable.

QUESTIONS

1. Is Christianity 'a repository of self-evidently humane and civilising values' today?

2. Is the doctrine of the Trinity really an antidote to the 'awesome totalitarian power of the Old Testament God'?

3. The Beatitudes spoke directly to Lara. What words in the Bible speak directly to you? Why?

4. Where is 'the spirit of narrowness ... worshipped as holy' in church and society today?

5. 'Neither gods nor peoples – only man.' Is that a good summary of the long-term effect of the Incarnation?

6. 'Nothing is more effective than poetry in making thoughts and sentiments memorable.' What are your favourite verses from the Psalms?

CHAPTER 6

The Fig Tree

Miracle and Judgement

THE POET

In early years Pasternak was much influenced by the passionate but idiosyncratic Christianity of Tolstoy, a friend of the family and frequent visitor to their home. Although he originally intended to be a musician, he eventually became a poet and a professional man of letters, making his living for much of his life by translating Western European masters for the huge Russian readership. You cannot translate any work without living with it, wrestling with it, forcing it to yield up its secrets, to disclose its inmost nature and to enrich you with a blessing, even if it cripples you. Pasternak was deeply marked by his acquaintance with the plays of Shakespeare. His version of *Hamlet* (1941) is the first of a brilliant series, which includes all the major tragedies.

The events of 1917 and the years that followed were characterised for Pasternak, as for many others, by the destruction of the right to private, non-political life, thought and emotions, and by the adoption of compulsory public optimism. By 1934, all creative writing in Russia had come to be controlled for the Communist Party by the Writers Union, which insisted on socialist realism as the only permissible literary tradition. The term 'socialist realism' implies contrast with the critical and poetic realism of Russian literature between roughly 1830 and 1880, the age of Pushkin, Lermontov, Gogol, Goncharov, Turgenev, Tolstoy and Dostoyevsky. It has, however, produced comparatively little which anyone with free access to other literature would choose to read for pleasure. With *Dr Zhivago*, Pasternak strikes his roots back into the deeper and richer soil of the great tradition.

During the postrevolutionary period, Pasternak retreated into writing lyric poetry and non-political plays, trying to inhabit and vindicate a purely private and personal world. Eventually he found it impossible to keep his personal life separate from the history of his country, and before he died he repudiated all that he had written in the twenties and thirties. He saw that lyric poetry was too limited and subjective to convey a vision, which is more than private, even if it is about personal privacy and integrity.

He wanted to produce a work of piety, to write the elegy of his own generation of intelligentsia of which he was the only surviving member, and who would otherwise have had no memorial. And he wanted a universal audience rather than the poetic coterie; 'fragmentary, personal poems', he said, 'are hardly suited to meditations on such obscure, new and solemn events. Only prose and philosophy can attempt to deal with them.'[1] So also, Yury Zhivago 'had dreamed of writing a book in prose, a book of impressions of life ... He was too young to write such a book; instead he wrote poetry. He was like a painter who spent his life making sketches for a big picture he had in mind.'[2]

One of the many peculiarities of *Dr Zhivago* is the absence not only of a plot in the Western sense, but also of a strong, positive, active hero. Yury Zhivago is, according to the best Russian, but not the Soviet literary tradition, a passive anti-hero. Things, events, the world, even women happen to him. Pasternak draws heavily on one aspect of the Christian view of man. Jesus learned obedience from the things which he suffered (Hebrews 5:8), and Pasternak constantly recalls both his obedience and his exceptional passivity in the face of passion, suffering and death, as preserved by the early church in the words of the Hebrew Scriptures: 'He was oppressed, and he was afflicted, yet he did not open his mouth; like a lamb that is led to the slaughter, and like a sheep that before its shearers is silent, so he did not open his mouth' (Isaiah 53:7). 'I gave my back to those who struck me, and my cheeks to those who pulled out the beard' (Isaiah 50:6). This is not the whole of the tradition but it is the strand which has been strongest in Russian folk culture and character since the time of Saints Boris and Gleb (martyred 1015) – meekness and the immense ability simply to absorb suffering and to survive.

Now it is very difficult to write a picaresque and plotless novel in which encounters are arranged along the life of the hero like beads on a thread and also to have an exceptionally passive hero. The clue is that this hero is a poet, who regards his task as being primarily 'transfiguration', the Christlike activity of handling suffering creatively, and using it as the raw material of glory. As things happen to him, he turns every significant encounter, usually a wound, a loss or a sacrifice, into art. He transmutes deaths and defeats into victories of the creative, life-giving spirit. Thus, at the book's climax, he lets Lara slip from his grasp, in order to have her forever as the poems which she inspires and which are published as *Zhivago's Poems* at the end of the novel.

Just as Pasternak developed from musician to poet to novelist, so Zhivago develops from doctor to poet to novelist. He had wanted to serve the world and cure its ills. He grows into wanting rather to transform it, to transfigure the cosmos by the creative use of language. All great art, all creativity in a bent world, comes with and through suffering. This common factor in the lives of artists is seen pre-eminently in Jesus as he acts creatively within a human life in Palestine, handling the stuff of life and of suffering, transfiguring it with his living word: 'Do this in remembrance of me' (1 Corinthians 11:24–25). *Poieite*, the word in our Greek New Testament which is usually translated 'do', might well be translated 'be creative', or even 'be a poet', and thus follow Jesus.

Pasternak, isolated, alone against his environment but confident of the rightness of his vision and judgement, and sustained through patches of doubt and despair by boundless hope of vindication, needed inner support. He came to find this in self-identification with Christ in his sufferings. At some stage in his life, in circumstances which remain hidden to us, he turned to Christ. There is just a hint of self-disclosure in 'Daybreak', of which the first two stanzas run:

> *You once meant everything to me.*
> *Then war came; life was all distorted.*
> *And in that long, long time no sound*
> *Nor rumour of you was reported.*
>
> *Years later once again your voice*
> *Disturbed me. I spent all night reading*
> *Your testament, and came to life*
> *As from a fainting fit unheeding.*

This sounds like the actual experience of one who, when questioned impertinently by a journalist about his conversion, replied, 'I am an atheist who has lost his faith', and 'When I sought a channel of communication with the creator, I was converted to Russian Orthodox Christianity. But, try as I might, I could not achieve a complete spiritual experience. Thus I am still a seeker.' Far from becoming a dogmatic loyalist, treating Christianity as an alternative ideology to Marxism, he remained a seeker to the end – like Tolstoy before him and Svetlana Alliluyeva (Stalin's daughter) after him, a Russian Orthodox seeker after truth. Faith for him meant the ability to be a free person, over against all serried ranks whatever, uncompromisingly himself as Jesus was.

It was not a matter of changing sides, and Pasternak was as embarrassed by attempts to enlist him as a Christian soldier in the Cold War as he had been infuriated thirty years earlier by the shouted behests of the Writers Union. 'Don't shout at me', he had protested, 'or at least, if you must shout, don't shout in unison'. He said to a visitor in the last year of his life:

> Scholars interpret my novel in theological terms. Nothing is further removed from my understanding. One must live and write restlessly, with the help of the new reserves that life offers. I am weary of this notion of faithfulness to a point of view at all costs. Life around us is ever-changing, and I believe that one should try to change one's slant accordingly – at least once every ten years.[3]

Beneath the humour we sense Pasternak's firm resolve, like Alyosha Karamazov, 'to love life rather than the meaning of it', and his powerful protest against all systems imposed by Pharisees, whether Christian or communist. He is content that in his novel the New Testament insights into 'free personality and life understood as sacrifice' should be offered to the reader as credible alternatives to the positive heroes and compulsory optimism of Soviet literature.

Only in the very last paragraph of the epilogue are the themes of isolation, passivity and suffering filled out by new notes of judgement, vindication and hope – just as they are in the Gospels:

> To the two aging friends [Gordon and Dudorov] sitting by the window, it seemed that this freedom of the spirit was there, that on that very evening the future had become

almost tangible in the streets below, and that they had themselves entered that future and would, from now on, be part of it. They felt a peaceful joy for this holy city [Moscow, but the reference is also to Jerusalem] and for the whole land and for the survivors among those who had played a part in this story and for their children and the silent music of happiness filled them and enveloped them and spread far and wide. And it seemed that the book in their hands knew what they were feeling and gave them its support and confirmation.[4]

The book is *Zhivago's Poems*, and Pasternak shows immense courage as well as self-assurance in making the meaning of the novel depend on the quality of the appended poems of which, after all, he is the real author and for which he must take ultimate responsibility. One of them is 'The Miracle'.

THE MIRACLE

In the Russian Orthodox Church the Monday in Holy Week is called 'Fig Tree Monday', after the dramatic miracle with which Jesus begins the day (Mark 11:12–25; cp. Matthew 21:18–22 and Luke 13:6–9). Pasternak retells the story for his contemporaries in the Soviet Union in the nineteenth of the Lara poems, entitled simply 'The Miracle'.

> *He trod the Jerusalem-Bethany road,*
> *Fatigued with fore-knowledge of sorrow to come.*
>
> *The squat prickly thorn bush stood scorched on the hillside,*
> *The reeds were unruffled, the air burning hot.*
> *O'er the cottage nearby the smoke hung without motion,*
> *The Dead Sea lay undisturbed, dormant and still.*
>
> *And in bitterness matching the salt bitter waters*
> *He walked on accompanied by a few clouds.*

By the dust-covered high road, to meet His disciples
At some obscure hospice, He strode into town.

So deep was He sunk in His own inmost thoughts
That the desolate field started smelling of wormwood.
The silence gripped all. He stood, lone, in the centre.
While, slumb'ring, the country lay flat as a sheet.
The heat and the desert, all fused with each other
And so did the lizards, the springs and the streams.

Not far from the roadside there towered a fig tree
Without any fruit – only branches and leaves.
He said to it, 'Tell me, what use are you to me?
What joy do you bring standing stiff as a post?

I crave food and drink, and you are infertile.
And this meeting with you is more thankless than granite.
How loathsome you are, and how lacking in talent!
Remain as you are, till the end of the age.'

A tremor of judgement ran down through the tree
Like the thunderbolt's flash through a lightning conductor.
The fig tree was cauterised right to its roots.

A moment's reprieve for the leaves and the branches,
The roots and the trunk, would have aided the laws
Of immutable nature to intervene for them.
But miracle is what it is; it is God.
When we are in turmoil, then through our confusion
It comes on us instantly and unawares.

The first four verses set a scene of desolation and isolation, of burning torrid heat, of human destitution and craving for refreshment. This scene is set out at length with many significant and pictorial details and with some poetic licence. For instance, the Dead Sea is not near or even visible from the road between Bethany and Jerusalem. But the next three verses, verses five to seven, describe an encounter, which is also a judgement. The tempo quickens. After the leisurely description, which matches the pace of a walk, there is a quick burst of action, very short, sharp and spare in its treatment, almost brutal and shocking in its power – and so is the Jesus it portrays. The hero of 'The Miracle' is the obverse of the anti-hero of 'Hamlet' (see chapter 7). He is active, vigorous, magisterial, judgemental, 'our hero strong and tender', he of whom they ask, 'Who then is this, that even the wind and the sea obey him?' (Mark 4:41). In fact this is an absolutely terrifying poem, unique in the series. Other commentators, with the significant exception of Elizabeth Jennings, simply ignore it.

What were Pasternak's sources for this poem? They were, first, his own experience of talent, creativity and fruitfulness, of human warmth and love on the one hand, and, on the other, of the barrenness and catatonic inhumanity of Soviet bureaucracy. Secondly, the Bible. Here, as in his accounts of Gethsemane, he basically follows Matthew's narrative, which he would have heard read in the liturgy of the Orthodox Church for the Monday in Holy Week – Fig Tree Monday: 'In the morning, when he returned to the city, he was hungry. And seeing a fig tree by the side of the road, he went to it and found nothing at all on it but leaves. Then he said to it, "May no fruit ever come from you again!" And the fig tree withered at once' (Matthew 21:18 – 19). If we ask where Matthew got this story from, the answer is, almost certainly, Mark.

> On the following day, when they came from Bethany, he was hungry. Seeing in the distance a fig tree in leaf, he went to see whether perhaps he would find anything on it. When he came to it, he found nothing but leaves, for it was not the season for figs. He said to it, 'May no one ever eat fruit from you again.' And his disciples heard it ...

In the morning as they passed by, they saw the fig tree withered away to its roots. Then Peter remembered and said to him, 'Rabbi, look! The fig tree that you cursed has withered.' Jesus answered them, 'Have faith in God. Truly I tell you, if you say to this mountain, "Be taken up and thrown into the sea", and if you do not doubt in your heart, but believe that what you say will come to pass, it will be done for you. So I tell you, whatever you ask for in prayer, believe that you have received it, and it will be yours.

'Whenever you stand praying, forgive, if you have anything against anyone; so that your Father in heaven may also forgive you your trespasses.' (Mark 11:12–14, 20–25)

You will have noticed the discrepancies. In Mark the tree is at a distance; in Matthew it is beside the road. In Mark, the change in the tree happens, so to speak, offstage, between one day and the next; in Matthew it is instantaneous and in full view of the disciples. And Matthew omits two awkward but essential items from Mark; first, the embarrassing but true remark that it was not the season for figs, and secondly the subsequent lessons about prayer and forgiveness. So Matthew has removed two things which would have made the story difficult for his first-century readers; but he foreshortens and heightens the miraculous element and the degree of discontinuity with the rest of what we know and expect of Jesus, in a way which makes his version more difficult for twentieth-century hearers, at least in the post-Enlightenment West.

If anything, Pasternak in his poem takes the development even further in a Matthean and miraculous direction. Not only is the penultimate verse deliberately brutal, but he adds a last verse of teaching, not as in the Gospels about faith and prayer but about miracles with the wonderfully sonorous take it or leave it line ,'*No chudo yest chudo i chudo yest Bog*' – (literally) 'But [a] miracle is [a] miracle and [a] miracle is God'. And he cannot resist that ironic reference to the laws of nature intervening. So much for scientific rationalism and indeed for scientific socialism! Incidentally Matthew also omits the dramatic and pictorial detail that the tree was withered 'to its roots' which Pasternak puts back in. There is a curious parallel here with his treatment of the Gethsemane story in 'Hamlet', where again he follows Matthew for the basic account but adds one detail of exceptional poetic value from Mark, namely the use of the word 'Abba' – 'Father'.

Now let us ask where Mark got the story. I think that there are two possibilities. The first is that he is writing up an actual event, probably a reminiscence of Peter who actually has a speaking part in the story – 'Look, Master, the fig tree you cursed has withered.' This is certainly a possible view, though I think that, as is usual in the transmission of anecdotes, there has been some foreshortening and telescoping of the lessons to be drawn from it. It seems to me to be probable that in the days before Passover Jesus saw a stricken and dying tree and used it, in the tradition of the great Hebrew prophets, as a symbol of God's judgement on his people for their hardness of heart and failure to produce the fruits of righteousness – mercy, judgement and truth. We should remember that during the interval between the two encounters with the tree in Mark's version, Jesus cleanses the temple. It is time for judgement to begin, and to begin with the house of God.

The other possibility, which cannot be wholly discounted, is that here we have a parable *of* Jesus which in the course of transmission has become a story *about* Jesus. That would solve the problem with 'the time of figs is not yet'. On the other hand there are other parables where the point is precisely that judgement comes at an inappropriate time – for example, 'the thief in the night' (Matthew 24:43–45) and 'the foolish virgins' (Matthew 25:1–13).

According to Luke Jesus told a parable about a fig tree in similar circumstances, though earlier in his ministry.

> A man had a fig tree planted in his vineyard; and he came looking for fruit on it and found none. So he said to the gardener, 'See here! For three years I have come looking for fruit on this fig tree, and still I find none. Cut it down! Why should it be wasting the soil?' He replied, 'Sir, let it alone for one more year, until I dig around it and put manure on it. If it bears fruit next year, well and good; but if not, you can cut it down.' (Luke 13:6–9)

Here the point of the story is that a stay of execution is granted; there is no gap between the story and the message of forgiveness.

The most we can say is that the first-century church preserved traditions about Jesus' use or uses of a fig tree for teaching purposes, whether as a straightforward parable (Luke), as an acted parable (Matthew), or as an example (Mark). And if we ask why he should have done so, where did he get the idea from, the answer is exactly the same as in the case of Pasternak, namely, from his own experience of being a free, loving and creative fully human person opposed by forces which were hard, dry and barren, which when you ask for bread will give you a stone (Matthew 7:9), and secondly of course from the Bible – in this case the Hebrew Scriptures, which Christians call the Old Testament.

Jesus would have known of the 'two baskets of figs placed before the temple of the LORD. This was after King Nebuchadrezzar of Babylon had taken into exile from Jerusalem King Jeconiah son of Jehoiakim of Judah, together with the officials of Judah, the artisans, and the smiths, and had brought them to Babylon. One basket had very good figs, like first-ripe figs, but the other basket had very bad figs, so bad that they could not be eaten.' The good ones were like the exiles in Babylon: 'I will set my eyes upon them for good, and I will bring them back to this land.' The bad ones are Zedekiah and the remnant of the people in the land and in Egypt – 'so bad that they cannot be eaten' (Jeremiah 24:1–6).

In the cultural consciousness of a Jew like Jesus, figs stood for people; they meant a nation, Israel under the judgement of God. To Pasternak in the twentieth century they also meant a nation, though this time they meant the Soviet Union, under the judgement of God.

In Pasternak's poem 'The Miracle', we see the extraordinary power and continuity of symbolism in an image from the early sixth century BC, preserved in Hebrew literature by the people of the book, reworked in a dramatic way by the re-creative genius of Jesus, transmitted from Aramaic, through Greek and Old Church Slavonic, to the mind of a modern poet, still putting out leaves for the healing of the nations and bearing fruit to refresh us and send us on our way, rejoicing it is true but also reminded of judgement as well as of mercy.

QUESTIONS

1. Have obedience and passivity been over-emphasised in Christianity? Are they now?

2. Which of the Gospel stories about the fig tree do you prefer? Why?

3. What aspects of the life of our own nation fall under the judgement of God?

4. How do we nourish the roots of creativity in ourselves and in others?

CHAPTER 7

The Garden of Olives

Identity, Obedience and Self-Surrender

HAMLET IN GETHSEMANE

All was hushed, I leaned against the door-post,
When I trod the scaffold of the stage,
Realising from the distant echo
What would come to pass in this, my age.

Night is aimed against me through a thousand
Black-eyed opera glasses in array.
Abba, Father, if it be possible,
Let this cup pass from me, now, I pray.

I embrace with love your stubborn purpose,
And I am content to play this part.
But another drama is impending.
And, this once, let me in peace depart.

But the road's end cannot be avoided,
And the order of the acts is sealed.
I'm alone. All drowns in Pharisaism.
Life is not a stroll across a field.

IDENTITY

Who, in this poem,[1] is 'I'?

As I read the lines, it is me; as you read them, it is you. 'I' is us – not simply us, but us impersonating an actor as he treads the boards. He in turn is impersonating Hamlet – a fictitious character, whose own 'I' is the 'I' of Shakespeare, in the guise of a historical character, the Prince of Denmark. Moreover, the poem purports to be by Yury Zhivago, the doctor-poet and hero of Pasternak's novel. He, too, is an 'I', a creator who is himself created by Boris Pasternak.

This is where we come back into the world of real persons. Not, however, without having gone through another, the key, impersonation. For Hamlet is portrayed as re-enacting in Denmark and retranslating for his age the role and persona of Jesus in Gethsemane. Pasternak's art shows us these persons, some in a variety of fictitious worlds, some in this world, all interpenetrated by Jesus. We dwell in him and he in us.

Part of Pasternak's message is the mutual interdependence of persons within a single corporate humanity. In this he is in agreement with our own John Donne – 'Noe man is an island ... I am involved in mankind.'[2] Both poets tap the same sources, the Scriptures of the Old and New Testaments and the best traditions of the church, which speak of the solidarity of humanity in Adam and in Christ and of the co-inherence of persons human and divine.

Sheer self-identification with Christ is impossible. The more Christ-like one is, the more he shrinks from it. So Pasternak in his poem goes through several stages – first identification with an actor and then with Hamlet. His approach is not oblique. On the contrary, he moves towards Jesus in a straight line; but his straight line towards the discovery of God takes him through the discovery of other persons. In writing up the drama of his own life – a drama in which the publication of *Dr Zhivago* and his enforced renunciation of the Nobel Prize was to be the crucial act – he begins in terms of the drama of Hamlet. Commenting on his own translation, he gives us the clue to his understanding of the play and to his surprising and striking use of 'Hamlet' to illustrate simultaneously his own life and the life of Jesus:

> *Hamlet* is not a drama of a weak character, but a drama of duty and self-denial. When appearance and reality are seen to diverge and are separated by a gaping chasm, it is of slight importance that the warning as to the world's falsity should come in a supernatural way, and Hamlet should be summoned to revenge by a ghost. It is of far greater importance that by the merest accident Hamlet should be chosen to sit in judgement on his age and become the servant of a remoter one. *Hamlet* is a drama of high vocation, of a call to heroic action in fulfilment of the hero's predestined task.

George Katkov, who quotes this excerpt in his note to Henry Kamen's translation of 'Hamlet', continues: 'It is the self-denial of Hamlet, who gives up his position in the society in which he was born, in order "to do the will of Him that sent him", that creates the poetic link with the Crucifixion and with Pasternak's own mission as he understood it.'[3]

For Pasternak the significance of Hamlet is that he is a man who has been sent a task by his father from heaven. (Søren Kierkegaard, who was himself a Dane, says that the ghost of Hamlet's father did not come back merely to say 'Hallo'.) From that moment, his course in life is steered between the demands of his absent father and his love for his mother. If it be true of Jesus and of Hamlet that their great love on earth is love for their mothers, it is equally true that they love and obey their fathers. It is the combination of love and obedience which enable them actually to achieve something in the world.

Like Jesus, Hamlet finds that the way leads through increasing isolation and betrayal by a friend who dies as a result of his own treachery in league with the ruler of this present age. Like Jesus, apparently perishing in vain, he concentrates at the end on re-conciliation, on appointing witnesses, and on re-establishing the kingdom. The parallels between the fictitious life of Hamlet and the real life of Jesus on the one hand, and between both of them and the fictional life of Yury Zhivago and the real life of Pasternak on the other, should not be drawn too far; but they may properly be pencilled in on our imagination as we return to the poem itself, and envisage the scene.

In verse 1, the Russian text suggests that the sound which dies down ('All was hushed') is the hum of chatter and expectancy in the theatre. It cannot only be that, because the play does not begin with Hamlet coming on to the stage. This must be the middle of Act 1, Scene 2. Horatio and Marcellus have set the scene for us, the Ghost has appeared, and now the entire entourage of Claudius, King of Denmark, and Gertrude the Queen, has entered to the sound of trumpets. Speech of great pomp and majesty concludes with Claudius:

> No jocund health that Denmark drinks today
> But the great cannon to the clouds shall tell,
> And the King's rouse the heaven shall bruit again
> Re-speaking earthly thunder. Come away.
> (Flourish. Exeunt all but Hamlet.)[4]

This must be the moment. Bereaved, tired, disgusted, torn, trying to grasp the meaning of his shattered universe, Hamlet prays a kind of prayer as he strains to catch the reflection of a still small voice coming back to him from the crowd of spectators, the audience of whom he requires sympathetic understanding and support.

> O, that this too too solid flesh would melt,
> Thaw, and resolve itself into a dew!
> Or that the Everlasting had not fix'd
> His canon 'gainst self-slaughter. O God! God!
> How weary, flat, stale and unprofitable
> Seem to me all the uses of this world!
> Fie on't! Ah, fie! 'tis an unweeded garden
> That grows to seed; things rank and gross in nature
> Possess it merely. That it should come to this![5]

Far from this anguish being met by benevolent sympathy, Hamlet's horror is only increased. He looks for human faces with eyes for windows of the soul, and sees with dread only the blank darkness of hard lenses, trained upon him like the barrels of a firing squad's rifles.[6] The first line of verse 2 is, in the Russian original of Pasternak's 'Hamlet', densely packed with hard 'Ah' sounds (*Na menya nastavlen sumrak nochi*).

This moment of intense isolation, loneliness, fear and dread is the crux of the poem, and the point at which Pasternak is at his most surprising and inventive. He cuts directly from identification with an actor playing Hamlet to identification with Christ being himself in Gethsemane:

> Abba, Father, if it be possible,
> Let this cup pass from me, now, I pray.

Basically Pasternak follows Matthew's account (Matthew 26:36–46), which he would have heard read in the Holy Week liturgy of the Russian Orthodox Church, but, quoting from memory, he harmonises this account with Mark's. The addition of 'Abba' (a child's 'my own father') (Mark 14:36) strengthens the cross-reference to 'Hamlet'. So does the image of the cup, which occurs in all the accounts of Gethsemane and which, for the persecuted eucharistic congregations of the early church, was a vivid symbol not only of joy and fellowship, but also of suffering and martyrdom (Matthew 26:27–29; Mark 14:23–25; Luke 22:17–18; cp. 1 Corinthians 11:25).

There is a cup in *Hamlet*, too – 'a chalice for the nonce'.[7] This is the poisoned cup, prepared by Claudius for Hamlet, but drunk by Gertrude. She dies for her son, albeit unwitting and in vain.[8] At the semi-liturgical climax of the drama it is the cup and not the sword which Hamlet holds in his hand as he dies, marked out for sacrifice at the place where his father's will and the way of the world collide.[9]

OBEDIENCE

Just as conflicting internal stresses had marked the earlier soliloquies of Hamlet, so it is the tension between the cost of sacrifice and the need for obedience which underlies Jesus' wrestling with his own spirit in Gethsemane. Almost always, when under extreme tension and not least on the cross, Jesus expresses his meaning in quotations from or references to the Psalms, the poetry of Israel. Here, it is the language and symbolism of Psalm 40 which informs his 'Thy will be done':

> *Sacrifices and offerings you have not desired,*
> *but a body you have prepared for me;*
> *in burnt offerings and sin offerings*
> *you have taken no pleasure.*
> *Then I said, 'See, God, I have come to do your will, O God'.*
> *(Psalm 40:6–8, as quoted in Hebrews 10:5–7)*

Pasternak conveys the hard, knobbly quality of the agony and the certainty of the outcome by a simple and brilliant effect:

> *I embrace with love your stubborn purpose,*
> *And ... But ... And ... But ... And ...*

In the Russian text, lines 10–14 begin with alternating 'ands' and 'buts'. This bold, even crude alternation skilfully reproduces that internal struggle between acceptance and rejection, which was characteristic of Hamlet. For Jesus, too, the struggle is real; but obedience to the Father is ultimately the controlling force. The end of the road, the strait way wide enough for one only, is reached; the narrow gate is accepted, gone through and triumphed over.

But to speak of that triumph immediately is to leap ahead of this particular poem into others in the same series.[10] For the moment, the hero, Jesus, like Hamlet, goes under, swamped in the formless chaos of a new universal flood, a new Red Sea, a new baptism. 'I'm alone. All drowns in Pharisaism' – the universal Pharisaism in Jerusalem at that fateful Passover, in the court at Elsinore and the rotten state of Denmark, in Zhivago's experience of the Civil War, of Pasternak's experience of the Writers' Union, of our experience, and of others' experience of us. It is a universal flood: Pasternak stresses that all drowns in Pharisaism, absolutely all.

In the very last line Pasternak surprises us again. He takes a simple and common Russian proverb and uses it to round off his poem with the wider meanings with which he has now invested it. To live life through, as Jesus did, and to bring life to perfection (for such is the full meaning of the phrase which I have translated so inadequately), to live right through life with all its disillusion and dissolution, including death itself, and to emerge into life eternal – this 'is not a stroll across a field'.

When Pasternak died in 1960, fifteen hundred people – peasants, workers and many students – ignored official disapproval and attended the funeral. He himself had expressly stated that he wished to be buried with the rites and ceremonies of the Orthodox Church. This was not allowed. Instead, friends and admirers filed past the coffin, while the pianist Sviatoslav Richter played funeral music on a small upright piano in Pasternak's house. Twelve young men bore the coffin to the graveyard, where it was buried at the foot of three pine trees.[11]

'Hamlet' had not yet been published in the Soviet Union, except secretly in *samizdat*. And yet, when it was read as Pasternak's memorial, it was taken up and recited in unison by the whole assembly, who recognised in it the essence of all that he had lived and died for[12] – to speak the truth in obedience to the poet's high calling, to be united with Christ and thus with all men of goodwill – a unity which is still partial but which is destined ultimately to triumph through suffering.

As he himself said in his *An Essay in Autobiography*, published in London a year before his death:

> It is more important in life to lose than to acquire. Unless the seed dies it bears no fruit. One must live tirelessly, looking to the future and drawing on the reserves of life which are created not only by remembering but also by forgetting.[13]

SELF-SURRENDER

In the last poem of the Holy Week cycle Pasternak had returned to the Garden of Gethsemane. Jesus' soliloquy there ends with the words:

> And for that fearful greatness I'll go down
> In voluntary torments to the grave.
>
> I shall go down and on the third day rise
> And, as the rafts upon the river float,
> To me for judgement like a string of barges
> The centuries will drift out of the night.

That last couplet completes the circle. 'Free personality and life understood as sacrifice' will be vindicated at last.

> To me for judgement like a string of barges
> The centuries will drift out of the night.

This is Pasternak's and Dr Zhigavo's last word. It is based on a remarkable visual image. We tend to envisage the centuries receding from us into the past so that, for example, the sixth century is further away from us than the sixteenth. Pasternak in his poem presents to us, as it were, the mind of Jesus leaping ahead to the end of all things and seeing the ages coming serenely towards him personally. There is something childlike and therefore divine about that.

This quality of being like a little child and therefore capable of entering the Kingdom of Heaven remained with Pasternak all his life. It recurs in the pages of *A Captive of Time: My Years with Pasternak*, the memoirs of Olga Ivinskaya, who was for many years his mistress and the original of Lara in *Dr Zhivago*.[14] It did not leave him on his deathbed – or rather deathbeds – since seven years before he died in 1960 he had already been laid at death's door after a heart attack, which inspired a very remarkable poem entitled 'In the Hospital'. Henry Gifford comments that the poems of Pasternak's last years:

> ... all testify to an inner peace. It is a very rare thing for poetry in this age continually to celebrate happiness and to express gratitude for life wholly unbidden. Such an attitude scarcely seems believable in a serious artist. Yet in Pasternak it is habitual and with the years this habit intensified.[15]

> *O Lord, how perfect are Thy works*
> *And wonderful, the sick man thought,*
> *Beds and the people and the walls,*
> *The dusk of death, the town at night.*

This is the first of four verses, which form the prayer with which the poem ends. It is a long narrative poem of thirteen verses, the origin of which is described in a letter, which Pasternak wrote to the Georgian poetess Nina Tabidze (17 January 1953) at the time of his illness.

> When it happened, and they took me away, and for five hours that evening I lay first in the casualty ward, and then for the night in the corridor of the usual vast and over-crowded city hospital, during the intervals between loss of consciousness and the onsets of nausea and vomiting I was possessed by such calm and bliss! ... And nearby everything followed such a familiar course, objects grouped themselves so distinctly, shadows fell so sharply! The long corridor, a whole verst, with the bodies of sleepers, sunk in twilight and silence, finished at a window on to the garden, with the inky murk of a rainy night and the reflection of the glare from a city, the glare of Moscow, beyond the tops of the trees. And this corridor, and the green glow of the lampshade on the

duty sister's table by the window, and the silence, and the shadows of the nurses, and the proximity of death beyond the window and at my back – all this in its concentration was such a fathomless and superhuman poem!

In the minute that seemed the last of my life, more than ever before I wanted to talk with God, to glorify what I saw, to catch and imprint it. 'Lord', I whispered, 'I thank Thee for having laid the colours so thickly and for making life and death such that Thy language is majesty and music, that Thou hast made me an artist, that creation is Thy school, that all my life Thou hast prepared me for this night.' And I rejoiced and wept from happiness.

The poem begins, like 'Hamlet', realistically – almost prosaically, almost impersonally in straightforward third person narration:

> He was laid down in the entrance hall,
> There was no room in the wards,
> The place smelt of iodine … etc.

Then, while remaining in the third person, the poem's point of view shifts to become that of the invalid, an invalid who observes every detail of a life which is reduced in scope but enriched in intensity, and who can tell from the way the nurse shakes her head that he is unlikely to come out of it alive. In these unpromising circumstances, *in extremis*, dying of a heart attack in a hospital corridor, he is overwhelmed with gratitude. The door keeps blowing open and he sees a maple bend in the wind, interpreting this movement 'as the tree's farewell bow to the dying man'. And then, for the prayer, there is a shift, as in 'Hamlet', to the first person singular. The dying man, the poet, Pasternak himself, is the subject of this eucharistic sacrifice of praise and thanksgiving.

'O Lord, How perfect are Thy works
And wonderful', the sick man thought,
'Beds and the people and the walls,
The dusk of death, the town at night.

While clutching at a handkerchief
After my sleeping draught I sob.
Tears of unending joy and grief
Obscure the vision of my God.

How sweet it is by this soft light
That scarcely reaches my bed-frame
To recognise myself, my fate,
As priceless gifts, marked with Thy name.

Now as I die in hospital,
Conscious of Thy warm hands' embrace,
Thou holdest me, Thy handiwork,
And hidest in Thy jewel case.'

I forebear to comment on the mastery of the verbalisa-
tion – the natural transition between ordinary everyday speech
and the sonorous rhythms and archaisms of Church Slavonic – the
perfect form for something which is so purely incarnational that
a banal event of contemporary urban life resounds with biblical
overtones. But I should like to look for a moment at that interior
attitude. In all the complexity of Pasternak's personal, literary and
political life (this event occurs just before the death of Stalin) there
is a kernel, revealed when approaching death strips off the outer
layers – a kernel of quiet, childlike confidence in a father's love,
and the simple assumption that I, even I, am a precious jewel in
the sight of God.

QUESTIONS

1. Who is 'I'?

2. Is 'Hamlet' a good example of the way in which literature can shed light on the biblical story? Can you think of others?

3. Hamlet's best insights into the human condition come out of depression. Give some biblical and personal examples of the same phenomenon.

4. 'It is more important in life to lose than to acquire.' Is it?

5. Can a poem like 'In the Hospital' help us, even if we were forgotten on a trolley in a draughty corridor, to face death?

CHAPTER 8

The Tree of Death

Cross and Passion

For to this you have been called, because Christ also suffered for you, leaving you an example, so that you should follow in his steps.

> 'He committed no sin,
>   and no deceit was found in his mouth.'

When he was abused, he did not return abuse; when he suffered, he did not threaten; but he entrusted himself to the one who judges justly. He himself bore our sins in his body on the cross, so that, free from sins, we might live for righteousness; by his wounds you have been healed. (1 Peter 2:21–24)

I have been fortunate enough in the course of my life to have met several saints, one of whom was Heinrich Grüber, Dean of Berlin Cathedral during the Third Reich. Incidentally, his colleague, Dean Lichtenberger of the Roman Catholic Cathedral, was a martyr; and it is good to remember these two brave and faithful men together. Grüber had the unique distinction, once Hitler had installed himself in the Chancellery, of paying a pastoral call on him simply as a neighbour to tell him that what he was doing was wrong. Hitler apparently was so astonished that, though he later had him imprisoned, he spared his life, rather as Herod spared the life of John the Baptist for a while and Stalin spared Pasternak. Be that as it may, Grüber survived; and when I met him in the 1950s he was sitting on the floor talking with a group of students. One of them said: 'You actually met Hitler. Wasn't he the devil incarnate?' And Grüber said: 'Oh no, he was just like any man (*jedermann*), that is to say, like Jesus.'

Now that says something about the incarnation, about the Word of God becoming flesh and taking our human nature upon him. But it also says something about the devil, whose tragedy is that he is not and cannot be incarnate. And the reason is this: that no one however corrupt is totally corrupt; no one embodies absolute negativity or the principle of non-existence; and, while most people believe partly in the devil and, indeed, act on that partial belief, no one believes wholly in him.

One person, the Blessed Virgin Mary, did believe wholly in God and put her total trust in his promised word, believed in him absolutely, mind, body and soul, with every fibre of her being, and opened herself so completely in trust and obedience to him that Jesus could, as the Athanasian Creed puts it, become 'Man, of the substance of his mother, born into the world'. No one is, or can be, so substantially united with the devil as that, for it is of the nature of the devil to be fragmented, partial, discarnate, as Ivan Karamazov sees in a revelatory hallucination, longing to become incarnate, to take flesh, 'too, too solid flesh', as a merchant's wife weighing at least eighteen stone; but he can't. Instead he has to content himself, or rather discontent himself, with apparently endless partial and fragmentary incarnations in those of us who with part of, perhaps with most of, but never with all our hearts and minds do evil in the world.

In the past few years we, like Macbeth, 'have supped full of horrors' – some of them abroad but still near at hand in Europe; others in distant lands afar but still in our world, in God's world; and all of them committed by human beings, all of them the result of that basic fault in human nature, which is traditionally called the fall and which afflicts us all. What then of those of whom St John says that they love darkness rather than light, because their deeds are evil (John 3:19)? Let me point to a strange phrase, which Jesus uses in a prayer for the disciples about Judas Iscariot, even while he is betraying him. Jesus calls him literally 'the son of destruction', and modern translations paraphrase this as 'a man who must be (or is destined to be) lost'. But why not take it at face value? If we do, it may shed some light on those who shed darkness in the world and whom we should seek rather to understand than to condemn, for God himself did not send his Son into the world to condemn the world but that the world might be saved through him (John 3:17).

Jesus does not call Judas, as one might expect, the father of destruction – in other words someone who causes mischief. He calls him the son of destruction, that is, the child or product of mischief. Surely that applies both to individual murderers and to mass murderers too. It is said that Hitler, even when master of continental Europe and at the height of his power, still sought in vain a remedy for the terrors of the dark, when he habitually woke from nightmares of being beaten and abused by his father. And certainly all the most destructive people I have come across in a more limited pastoral experience than Heinrich Grüber, have, I realise sometimes only with hindsight, been children of destruction. Not for nothing did Jesus reserve his strongest condemnation, indeed by implication the death penalty, for those who abuse little children and of whom it might be said that it would have been better if they had been thrown into the sea with millstones around their necks (Matthew 18:6).

That is one of the reasons why the story of the massacre of the innocents by Herod in Bethlehem is an essential part of the Christmas story, and celebrated, if that is the right word, on December 28. There are plenty of non-sentimental reasons for having a special concern for children at Christmas time, and they have to do with the underlying need for the incarnation as well as with the form it took, with the power of darkness as well as with the coming of the light. And again it is Ivan Karamazov who points to the futility of finding satisfaction in the prospect of hell as a place of eternal punishment for child abusers. 'What good to me is a hell for the oppressors?' he says. 'The children have already been tortured.' This point cannot be answered by words; it can only be met by deeds and by personal intervention.

In chapter 1 we were looking at the tree of the knowledge of good and evil in the Garden of Eden. It reminded us that a benevolent and loving God is the Creator and maker of the whole world, which is a fallen world, a world which falls short of its potential for glory because the men and women, to whom God has entrusted it, are too immature, too frightened, too lacking in faith and hope and love to trust God to have got it right; too sinful to be a faithful steward or a loyal spouse, or even much of a snake-charmer. We are too anxious to be able to wait for fruit and time to ripen, so we take the shortcuts of robbery and violence, even the torture of little children; sin leads us to crimes against both nature and our fellow human beings.

However, as the old Russian proverb puts it, 'God sees the truth but waits'. He waits for the fullness of time and then he comes, this time not to Paradise but to Paradise lost, and not *to* Adam but *in* Adam. As God and Man in Jesus Christ he comes into a fallen humanity and a fallen world to do two things. One is to take responsibility for the fall of man – he bore our sins in his own body on the tree, as St Peter says (1 Peter 2:24); the other is to take responsibility for the creative activity of God – God who on the cross was in Christ, reconciling the world to himself, as St Paul says (2 Corinthians 5:19).

Now this, which is the essence of the gospel according to St Paul – that God was in Christ upon the cross – was an absolutely scandalous notion when it was first written to the infant church at Corinth, consisting as it did largely of Gentile converts to Judaism, God-fearing men and women who had been enthralled by the beauty and majesty, the clarity and sublimity of the Jewish belief in one transcendent God, and brought out of pagan darkness into monotheistic light long before they became Christians. To many of them it was scandalous now to be asked to believe that God Almighty, the Lord, Creator and Sustainer of the Universe, should be within human suffering, degradation, shame and agony, acute physical pain and spiritual darkness, as well as outside it, overarching it, holding it and all things in his hands.

This paradoxical belief, which is the clue to the glory of God and man and which the evangelists and apostles saw in the cross, was not then, and never has been since, widely accepted. One of the reasons why it has been accepted at least within the Christian tradition *at all* (and that is what needs explaining) is that there is in this appalling act of cruelty and injustice surprisingly enough something fitting and just; there is an appropriateness – what Charles Dickens called a 'universal dovetailing' – about it, which answers a deep-seated moral demand, which we experience at a somewhat deeper level than conscious thought, and at a far deeper level than our habitual religious reflexes and our earnest attempts, like the elder brother of the Prodigal Son, to be good boys and only say nice things about our father.

We ought rather to take as our example the prodigal son, and the importunate widow, and the violent men who take the Kingdom of Heaven by force; we ought rather to learn from the psalmist, from Jacob, Jonah, Job and Jeremiah, (the great J's), and from the awful cry of dereliction of our Lord Jesus Christ, to open our hearts and our lungs to God, to cry out and express ourselves, our angry, lonely, empty, longing selves, and thus give him something real and natural to take and break and transform, as he turned Jonah's anger, his petty pique and spite, into the revelation of his love for the whole city of Nineveh, 120,000 persons and besides much cattle!

All things are possible to those who have faith; and we can say what we really think of God to God, if only we believe that God, who has the knowledge of good and evil (that is to say, power over both), can work sacramentally with anything which is genuine. 'The wrath of man shalt thou turn to thy praise' (Psalm 76:10). There is only one thing which God cannot turn or transform, because it is nothing – no thing – and that is what the Old Testament calls vanity – emptiness, façade, pretence and pretentiousness. The superficial surface of convention obscures for us the depth both of human faith and of divine compassion.

We must get below the surface, and here I find artists often help us as much as theologians; composers, novelists and painters as much as preachers. They cut deep and 'tell it slant'.[1] We can only believe that God was in Jesus on that awful tree when we suffer enough and when we care enough about suffering in the world to want to believe in the depths of our souls that it really was God himself who suffered the worst that the world can work on anyone, to want to believe this because we first believe that the world which does the crucifying, the world in which we sin and in which we suffer, is his world which he made.

The first article of belief is: 'We believe in God, the Father Almighty, Maker of heaven and earth, of all that is seen and unseen.' The second is: 'And in one Lord Jesus Christ ... through him all things were made.' The church found this astonishing insight very difficult to formulate, and we find it very difficult to understand that Jesus of Nazareth should be the agent of God the Creator in setting up and keeping going the whole world, that as St John said: 'Without him not one thing came into being' (John 1:3). But those who crucified Jesus are not different or separate from us; they represent us. When they cried out: 'Crucify him, crucify him', they were acting on that very same insight, expressing our vexation with God, our primordial rage and revolt against the Father, our righteous indignation at a Creator, who has made a world in which pain and suffering and grief are a possibility, let alone an actuality, and who has put us in it with no way out but death.

They crucified him not because they misunderstood him, but because they understood him all too well, when he said: 'The Father and I are one' (John 10:30). Jesus was not crucified for lying; many fanatics have claimed identity with God and gone scot-free. Who has ever been crucified for lying? Crucifixion, total physical, mental and spiritual destruction, is reserved for the one who tells the truth and who tells it credibly, because he is and does the truth, as Plato prophesied: 'When the perfectly good man comes, he must be crucified.'

So it was people who perceived in their hearts that Jesus was one with the Almighty Father, because they had seen with their own eyes the Godlikeness of his life in the days of his flesh; such people crucified him, not for claiming to be God but for being God. In him God had come back to do what Adam would never do unaided, namely, to take responsibility for the world, to be stretched out and torn apart by the tension between the creation as it is and the creation as it should be, to fill up in his own person the gap left by the shortfall, to pay with his own life poured out, like pieces of silver, the price of sin.

With his torso stretched out to bridge the gap between earth and heaven and his arms flung wide to embrace us all, he himself bore our sins in his own body on the tree. He bore our griefs and carried our sorrows and upon him was laid the iniquity of us all. More than that, and this is the mystery of dereliction, he bore God's grief, which by a merciful providence we can only glimpse from afar and are prevented from understanding, just as the healing power of forgetfulness prevents us from ever remembering the pangs and anguish of our own birth. There is a strength, Pasternak says, which comes not only from remembering but also from forgetting.

The psychologist C. J. Jung, who was the son of a Swiss Protestant pastor, says that it is not so much a matter of man in Christ paying the price of sin to the Father, in order to be set free from the consequences, as God in Christ making reparation to man for a world in which sin and suffering are not only possible but inevitable. If the man who dies on the cross is not God himself, then the cross is simply one tragedy among many, and God loses even more moral credibility. That verges on the blasphemous – but blasphemy is an attitude and a tone of voice rather than a form of words; and I believe that that insight can be offered up as part of our sacrifice of praise and thanksgiving with piety and devotion, rather as it is strangely enough in the Thirty-Nine Articles.

As every schoolboy – or at least every ordinand – knows, Article 2 is mistaken in saying that Christ 'truly suffered, was crucified, dead, and buried to reconcile his Father to us', whereas it should read, 'to reconcile us to his Father'. But should it? Did not our fathers in 1562 prophesy more than they knew? Did they not get it right by accident? Did not Christ indeed die upon the tree 'to reconcile his Father to us', after all? It is worth considering. For it was fitting, as the writer of the letter to the Hebrews put it, 'that God, for whom and through whom all things exist, in bringing many children to glory, should make the pioneer of their salvation perfect through sufferings' (Hebrews 2:10). It was appropriate that the Son of Man, when he was seen to be the Son of God, should suffer. It was a moral necessity and a divine obligation. It was not inevitable, but it was a conscious choice.

We can begin to believe this horrible and glorious paradox because, when we are given faith by grace to go down deeply into our own sufferings and those of others, we can see that it is fitting, as the risen Christ himself taught the two disciples at Emmaus, that the Christ of God should suffer and so enter into his glory (Luke 24:26). He entered his glory in this way and in no other, on this tree and no other.

Sydney Carter makes the same point with an edgy irony in his song 'It Was on a Friday Morning' on the lips of the penitent thief:

> It was on a Friday morning
> That they took me from the cell,
> And I saw they had a carpenter
> To crucify as well.
> You can blame it on to Pilate,
> You can blame it on the Jews,
> You can blame it on the Devil,
> It's God I accuse.
> It's God they ought to crucify
> Instead of you and me,
> I said to the carpenter
> A-hanging on the tree.
>
> You can blame it on to Adam,
> You can blame it on to Eve,

You can blame it on the Apple,
But that I can't believe.
It was God that made the Devil
And the Woman and the Man
And there wouldn't be an Apple
If it wasn't in the plan.

To hell with Jehovah,
To the carpenter I said,
I wish that a carpenter
Had made the world instead.
Goodbye and good luck to you,
Our ways will soon divide.
Remember me in heaven,
The man you hung beside.
It's God they ought to crucify
Instead of you and me,
I said to the carpenter
A-hanging on the tree.[2]

QUESTIONS

1. Is it true that the devil cannot be fully incarnate?

2. Even in Judas?

3. What does it mean to say that it was fitting that Christ should die on the cross?

4. 'I wish that a carpenter had made the world instead.' Do you?

CHAPTER 9

Words from the Tree (1)

Emptiness, Forgiveness and the Promise of Paradise

1. DEATH ON A CROSS

Let the same mind be in you that was in Christ Jesus,

> who, though he was in the form of God,
>> did not regard equality with God
>> as something to be exploited,
> but emptied himself,
>> taking the form of a slave,
>> being born in human likeness.
> And being found in human form,
>> he humbled himself
>> and became obedient to the point of death –
>> even death on a cross. (Philippians 2:5–8)

'He emptied himself' is one of the most difficult phrases of the New Testament to understand, because if Jesus really did empty himself of all that it means to be in the form of God, then it is difficult to see how he could have achieved what he did achieve on earth. Moreover, the other great hymn in the New Testament about the incarnation (Colossians 1:15–20) appears to say exactly the opposite: 'For in him all the fullness of God was pleased to dwell.' Where Philippians speaks of emptiness (*kenosis*), Colossians speaks of fullness (*pleroma*). Can they both be right? I think they can; and to illustrate that – not to prove, but to illustrate – I want to take an example from my own experience in what Boris Pasternak calls 'a far and humble likeness' of our Lord's experience.

Before I was called to the ministry I trained as an interpreter, and I have practised that trade intermittently throughout my life. Simultaneous interpretation is a fascinating craft. It consists of receiving one set of signals by listening and transmitting another set by speaking – all at the same time. People are kind enough to admire it and even to say it is miraculous, but it isn't. It is a learned human skill like any other; and it depends upon the ability to do more than one thing at a time, which is a common, indeed a universal, faculty.

What does it feel like to interpret? Well, you don't feel very much at all because you have to concentrate so hard on hearing the message and on reproducing it faithfully. But you do feel intensely alive. You are not in any way diminished. You do not renounce any of your faculties, anything of your personality or character, any of what makes you you. What you do do is to become a channel, as we pray in the well-known chorus: 'Make me a channel of your peace.'

An interpreter opens herself so that the message can flow through. It does not flow through unchanged. It exchanges one language, one form, for another; but – and this is the real test – the content, the essential message, the substance of the word remains the same. This can only be done if the interpreter empties herself of all that could obstruct either the exercise of her craft or the content of the message – self-consciousness, self-assertion, self-will. An interpreter is most herself when she renounces self and gives herself wholly to the task. And the strange thing is, as I can testify from experience, that emptying oneself to exercise a skill like interpreting is fulfilling in a way that being full of oneself is not.

It is not only interpreters who have this experience. Edith Reyntiens, a Russian Orthodox icon painter, writes as follows: 'the process of painting an icon every time is a process of self-emptying, a sort of Kenosis ... We struggle against our own ambition, our own notions of what would look good.' She speaks here not of creativity for, strictly speaking, only God can create. She speaks instead of inspiration, of opening up the channels through which the Spirit can flow. This is consonant with the command of Jesus to his disciples and to us, not to fulfil ourselves, but to deny ourselves, to take up our cross and to follow him – that is to say, to renounce self and give oneself wholly to the task.

Is this not what Jesus, the word of God made flesh, does both in the incarnation and upon the cross? At least something like it, I dare to think. It is not that he has no character, no personality, no nature of his own. That would be one heresy. Nor is it that he has no will of his own; that would be another. His will is not obliterated, but it is wholly and constantly aligned to the will of his Father in heaven, with whom by the Spirit he is constantly linked in prayer.

Perhaps we can say, taking our text not as a doctrinal treatise but as what it is, a poem, that Jesus emptied himself, not so much of his divine attributes as of those elements of fallen human nature, self-love, self-absorption, self-sufficiency, self-assertion, which get in the way of being filled by the Spirit of God, which is that fullness of God of which St Paul speaks, the whole being and power of God.

We get a foretaste, an indication, a preview of this pattern already at the annunciation, when Mary opened herself to the message of the angel, offered herself in total obedience and abandonment to the divine will and became ready to be filled with

God incarnate in her womb. She did this in the days of Octavius Caesar, just at the moment in human history when Roman emperors were beginning to grasp at divinity, taking the titles 'Divus' and 'Augustus'; and it is worth recalling that Paul was writing to the Philippians from a prison cell in Rome under the Emperor Nero, so that the contrast between the self-emptying of Jesus and the self-aggrandisement of one who 'regarded equality with God as something to be seized and exploited' was very bold. Then, as now, it is the incarnation of Almighty God as a helpless babe in the womb of a virgin which is the antidote to overweening pride and political power and a sign of hope to the humiliated and oppressed, to them that walk in darkness and in the shadow of death.

A poem may have more than one meaning at a time; and here, though we could treat this passage as if it were primarily about the incarnation, we ought to note that it is also about the atonement, about Christ pouring out his life as the suffering servant of God. It is just as much a Good Friday chorale as it is a Christmas carol. In writing to the Colossians, Paul makes that direct connection: 'in him all the fullness of God was pleased to dwell, and through him God was pleased to reconcile to himself all things, whether on earth or in heaven, by making peace through the blood of his cross' (Colossians 1:19–20). Crib and cross are hewn from the same wood; Christmas Day and Good Friday are morning and evening of the same day; reconciliation is the reason for the incarnation.

But what is reconciliation? It is a rare concept and a rare word even in the Greek New Testament. At its heart is a common word meaning 'other' or 'different'; in common use it came to mean change or exchange, as in changing money; behind it lies the view in the Hebrew Scriptures that no true change comes about without sacrifice. So in the incarnation the otherness of the divine meets the otherness of the human. It does not repudiate it; on the contrary, it accepts it and affirms it, as the *Te Deum* says in a phrase which strikes us as quaint but which was immeasurably reassuring in late antiquity with its horror of bodies, especially of women's bodies: 'When thou tookest upon thee to deliver man thou didst not abhor the Virgin's womb' – *non horruisti Virginis uterum.*

Some modern translations of this wonderful phrase are unnecessarily and gratuitously feeble. It is not an insult to women; it is the affirmation and acceptance of the otherness of humanity by God himself. But at Calvary the otherness of God meets the otherness not only of the flesh he has created in his own image but also of human sinfulness. Our repudiation of God contrasts strongly with God's acceptance of us. It is on the cross that the great exchange takes place, not without sacrifice. With hindsight it can be seen to be the logical conclusion and the consummation of the nativity; it is what must happen when God comes to his own and his own receive him not (John 1:11 AV/KJV).

2. FATHER, FORGIVE THEM

When they came to the place that is called The Skull, they crucified Jesus there with the criminals, one on his right and one on his left. Then Jesus said, 'Father, forgive them; for they do not know what they are doing.' And they cast lots to divide his clothing. And the people stood by, watching; but the leaders scoffed at him, saying, 'He saved others; let him save himself if he is the Messiah of God, his chosen one!' The soldiers also mocked him, coming up and offering him sour wine, and saying, 'If you are the King of the Jews, save yourself!' There was also an inscription over him, 'This is the King of the Jews.' (Luke 23:33–38)

The Evangelist simply says, in one word, 'they crucified' him; he does not go into details or add his own emotions as commentary upon the bare fact. A Gospel is epic, not lyric; emotion is there but by the time it is written down it has been recollected in tranquillity, in that peace of God which surpasses understanding and which was the experience of the early church. But that peace had been bought at a price and the first Christians knew the value of the coinage because crucifixion, for all that each instance was uniquely tragic and agonising, was an everyday event in the outlying provinces of the Roman Empire. We, rightly, look back on the crucifixion and are astonished at its uniqueness, at the cross of Christ 'towering o'er the wrecks of time'. But for Luke and his readers it had something of the banality, the sickening, loathsome banality of rape and murder in Darfur, bombings in Baghdad, burnings under Mary or bowellings under Elizabeth. It is what we do to each other when we get the chance.

But – and this is the secret of the incarnation – if on the one hand the death of Jesus is ordinary, if it is the last term in a series in which he shares fully the life of humankind on earth, on the other hand it is extraordinary; and to indicate this Luke tells his apparently straightforward epic tale in language filled with allusions to Psalm 22 and to Isaiah 53:12, where we read, 'He poured out himself to death, and was numbered with the transgressors.' For the Roman soldiers and the authorities, to place Jesus between two hardened and outcast criminals was both a malicious insult and also a vain attempt to make a lynching look legitimate. For Luke it was the fulfilment of a prophecy and a sign pointing beyond the scaffold to the Suffering Servant of God himself.

Isaiah 53:12 goes on: 'yet he bore the sin of many, and made intercession for the transgressors.' We will see later how that intercession operates for one of the two criminals, but it is the irony of the cross that the transgressors for whom God's servant intercedes are not just condemned criminals but the respected rulers of his own people and the agents of Roman justice. The crucifixion is a judgement on them; and later in the preaching of Peter, lest anyone should still be tempted by the slander that it was the Jews alone who bore responsibility for the death of Jesus, we note the full scope of that condemnation. 'For in this city, in fact, both Herod and Pontius Pilate, with the Gentiles and the peoples of Israel, gathered together against your holy servant Jesus, whom you anointed, to do whatever your hand and your plan had predestined to take place' (Acts 4:27–28). It is Herod and Pontius Pilate, the people of Israel and the Gentiles, who, because they killed 'the Author of life' (Acts 3:15), are revealed as criminals who offend against fundamental laws.

From Adam to the present day we have been turning upside down the laws of God and nature, destroying each other, polluting the earth, perverting each true and decent impulse; and nowhere is this seen more clearly than in the collusion of arms with power which comes to a head in the crucifixion. Again Peter quotes Psalm 2 when he prays:

> Sovereign Lord, who made the heaven and the earth, the sea, and everything in them, it is you who said by the Holy Spirit through our ancestor David, your servant:
>
>> 'Why did the Gentiles rage,
>>   and the peoples imagine vain things?
>> The kings of the earth took their stand,
>>   and the rulers have gathered together
>>   against the Lord and against his Messiah.' (Acts 4:24–26)

It is a public and political event and it avails for public and political life. But the death of Jesus is personal and individual too. There is so much in this dying, the nakedness, the indignity, the pain, even the words he utters, which are so intimate that the very fact that it happens publicly is an added horror. There is at the very least a monstrous impropriety in the element of display, which was an essential part of crucifixion, whereby fellow men were pinned up on boards like butterflies so that others might indulge their sadistic and voyeuristic impulses by watching them flutter. It takes something as foul and loathsome and as intimate, as well as public, as the crucifixion to deal as God has done in Christ with every perversion of the human spirit; and that extends from the most secret vices to the arena of international politics – the sins of the world as well as the sin of the world.

'There was also an inscription over him, "This is the King of the Jews"' (Luke 23:38). By a double irony that label told the truth; it was presented as false, as another cruel mocking slander both of Jesus and the Jews, but Pilate prophesied what he did not know, though his wife had begun to guess it in her troubled dreams and his centurion was now standing where the light would eventually enlighten him.

At the centre of Luke's crowded scene, where the intensely intimate secret and hidden things of the heart intersect with politico-military events and ecclesiastical intrigue at the world historical level, there is a young carpenter; and because the world is turned upside down by sin, he is not hammering and nailing, he is being hammered and nailed, sharing the fate not only of his fellow men but also of the uncomplaining timber, which also dies for men, though unwitting. His tormentors are temporary and part-time carpenters of a kind. And whenever and by whatever means human beings, living subjects, are treated by their fellows as if they were inanimate objects, the same topsy-turvy pattern of the crucifixion is traced out again in lesser Calvaries.

It is the beginning of the end of his passion. He still has life and breath and consciousness. He continues his work and ministry even to the end. What is his essential work on earth? It is the maintenance through prayer in all circumstances of unbroken unity with the Father. And so he prays. The action reveals the man himself and his kinship with God. He prays for forgiveness; and that is not something we should take for granted, or we lapse into the cynical blasphemy of Voltaire: *'Dieu pardonnera, c'est son métier* – God will forgive, after all it's his job.' It isn't; his job is making things. Father and Son are Creator and carpenter. Forgiveness is a bonus – it is undeserved, unmerited; it is pure grace. Like the quality of mercy,

> *It is not strained.*
> *It droppeth as the gentle rain from heaven*
> *upon the place beneath. It is twice blessed.*
> *It blesses him that gives and him that takes.*
> *'Tis mightiest in the mightiest; it becomes*
> *the throned monarch better than the crown …*
> *It is an attribute to God himself.*[1]

And the poor, bloodstained, naked carpenter, cleated to the crossbar, manifests this Godlike attribute to all who will receive it. Some have said that the clause 'for they know not what they do' limits the scope of forgiveness to the ignorant. But does it? St Peter in his preaching, for all the clarity and vigour of the condemnation, pleads ignorance on the part of every Jew and Gentile. 'And now, friends, I know that you acted in ignorance, as did your rulers' (Acts 3:17). Had he not acted in ignorance himself, when he denied Jesus, to whom he was as close as any? For who has really understood the length and breadth and depth of anything, of any subatomic particle let alone of the love of God in Christ Jesus? We know enough to be guilty; and we are ignorant enough to be forgiven. That is what the fisherman says; and he knows, because he learnt it from the carpenter.

3. TODAY YOU WILL BE WITH ME IN PARADISE

One of the criminals who were hanged there kept derid-
ing him and saying, 'Are you not the Messiah? Save yourself
and us!' But the other rebuked him, saying, 'Do you not fear
God, since you are under the same sentence of condemnation? And we indeed have been condemned justly, for we are
getting what we deserve for our deeds, but this man has done
nothing wrong.' Then he said, 'Jesus, remember me when
you come into your kingdom.' He replied, 'Truly I tell you,
today you will be with me in Paradise'. (Luke 23:39 – 43)

The verse which we have just been considering – 'Father, forgive them; for they do not know what they are doing' – does not
occur in many of the most ancient manuscripts of the Bible. And
yet many scholars believe that they were original. Perhaps at some
point in the second century there was a scribe who simply could
not believe either that Jesus had prayed that the Jews would be
forgiven or, if he had so prayed, that the Father had answered his
prayer; so those words were left out. Much of the early development of the Christian church was a response to the almost total
destruction of the Jewish nation, religion and capital city of Jerusalem in AD 70 and its apparently total annihilation in the first
attempt at a final solution of AD 135.

From the earliest times Christian writers have found it difficult to believe that Jesus meant the Father to forgive the Jews;
and Christian anti-Semitism has been a persistent shame and
scandal up to the present day. Perhaps we, living in the shadow
of the Shoah, of the latest attempt at a final solution, are better
placed than intervening generations to meditate on God's choice
of Israel, on his faithfulness to his first love and on his mercy to
the thousandth generation of those who love him. But behind
the problem which led our second-century scribe to smooth his

passion by omitting a problematic verse lies a deeper offence and mystery: that of forgiveness itself – not just of forgiving the Jews for their part in the crucifixion of the Messiah, but of forgiving at all. It is offensive to forgive too easily – to mumble 'It's alright' when it isn't, or 'Never mind' when you ought to mind. The cross is a permanent reminder of the cost to God of this mysterious transaction, called variously forgiveness, acceptance, expiation, or atonement. Dietrich Bonhoeffer consistently warned against the temptations of 'cheap grace'.

The offer can be accepted or it can be rejected; and St Luke dramatises the choice and its consequences in the episode of the two robbers, who both begin – according to Matthew and Mark – by joining in the general mockery of Jesus, taking their cue from their rulers: 'If he is the Messiah of God, let him save himself.' Satan in the wilderness had tested Jesus at the start of his ministry with one 'if': 'If you are the Son of God'; and Jesus had stood that test. Now the value of that first victory becomes apparent as at the end of his ministry he stands the same test in even more difficult circumstances and wins his first victory as Saviour *in extremis*, revealing even on the gallows the power of God to save, the meaningfulness of human choice and, therefore, of human life itself.

Rembrandt in his famous late etching of the crucifixion[2] worked and reworked the treatment, hacking away directly at the plate itself to produce great rays of darkness across all the scene except for a little light on Jesus and one malefactor. It is a scene of contrast and of stark choice; for all the kindness and tenderness of the word to the penitent thief, there is no touch of pathos or of sentimentality here. It is a hard gospel and a strong one – a battle between light and darkness, life and death, condemnation and salvation. In that battle one man changes sides as the model, prototype and forerunner of all who since that moment have turned from sin to the crucified Christ and put their trust in him.

Rembrandt van Rijn. Christ Crucified between the Two Thieves: *The Three Crosses*. Etching, 1653. Courtesy of The Pierpont Morgan Library / Art Resources, New York.

This malefactor begins with an instinctive faith and religious sense: 'Do you not fear God?' They are the prerequisite of repentance, and without them no further step is possible. Then he responds to something he perceives in Jesus and admits both his own criminality and the justice of his punishment. Of course there must be reasons and extenuating circumstances, and of course the punishment is barbarously exaggerated, for what crime could possibly deserve crucifixion? But these are armchair arguments; a man in need of salvation does well to prefer justification by faith to justification by self. Self-justification gets you nowhere. In a few words the penitent thief trusts in God, confesses his own sin, acknowledges Jesus' innocence and recognises him as king.

Perhaps he had read the ironic superscription recorded in Greek by Luke as 'This is the King of the Jews', and he had seen more deeply into its essential meaning than had those whose only response was mockery and cynicism. More likely it was the Aramaic form 'Jesus of Nazareth, King of the Jews' he read, for he addressed Jesus by name. This is the only place in the Gospels where anyone simply addresses our Lord as 'Jesus', the name which is above every name and which, after all, is a simple sentence meaning 'God saves'.

We may well meditate on what the Saviour's words would mean to the malefactor; but what must it have meant to Jesus to be called by name by a fellow human being, a fellow sufferer on the cross? Kindness and love of neighbour were being offered by the thief, like a cup of cold water to a thirsty man, a cup which, as Jesus had promised, would receive its reward. He said, 'Jesus, remember me when you come in your kingdom.' In a very short time he has completed the course of Christian discipleship, literally at the feet of the master. As one commentator has said, 'he has grown so close to Jesus that he has outdistanced even the most intimate of the disciples with their two or three years' close companionship and special training.'[3]

Jesus said to him, 'Truly I tell you, today you will be with me in Paradise.' The answer exceeds the request for, as St Augustine taught, God is always ready to give more than we either desire or deserve. It is not for us to speculate about the nature of Paradise; it is enough to recognise with St Paul that it is 'to be with Christ' (Philippians 1:23). Strictly speaking 'in Paradise' adds nothing to 'you will be with me'; but it was an exquisite touch of personal pastoral care by the good shepherd to one lost sheep, in speaking to a man tortured like himself by thirst and anguishing under the burning noonday sun, to add to the greater promise ('you will be with me') the lesser but more pictorial and therefore more easily grasped 'in Paradise' – in a cool, enclosed park or pleasure garden, all green leaves and cool shade and running water, like Eden before the fall.

Our thoughts should rather turn in quiet and grateful trust to the possibility and seriousness of sincere and effective repentance for sin and the knowledge that 'any glib or superficial confidence ... is ruled out by the spectacle of the other robber, scratched right out in Rembrandt's etching, dying defiantly within reach and earshot but out of touch with his Saviour.'[4]

QUESTIONS

1. Do you understand what you are asking when you sing, 'Make me a channel of your peace'?

2. In what ways is the incarnation a challenge to the totalitarian claims of states?

3. Should forgiveness be limited to those who do not know what they are doing?

4. Do you not fear God?

CHAPTER 10

Words from the Tree (2)

Adoption, Dereliction and Thirst

4. HERE IS YOUR SON, HERE IS YOUR MOTHER

Meanwhile, standing near the cross of Jesus were his mother, and his mother's sister, Mary the wife of Clopas, and Mary Magdalene. When Jesus saw his mother and the disciple whom he loved standing beside her, he said to his mother, 'Woman, here is your son.' Then he said to the disciple, 'Here is your mother.' And from that hour the disciple took her into his own home. (John 19:25–27)

Now comes what seems to be an interlude – personal, domestic, gentle and warmhearted. Such is the restraint of the Evangelist that, apart from the stage direction 'standing near the cross of Jesus', we might almost forget the circumstances in which these simple words are spoken and these family arrangements made.

None of the Evangelists is a sensationalist; that is to say, they do not attempt to convey the actual sensations of crucifixion. Perhaps their first readers lived so intimately with horror that it was not necessary. Perhaps it is only those who are shielded from suffering who produce and enjoy a culture in which violence and pain are purveyed and described in detail. Gilbert Murray's words on classical Greek literature also apply to the Gospels. He speaks of the crowded active life as husbands, farmers, local politicians and soldiers in Bronze Age warfare of Aeschylus, Sophocles and Euripides:

> It is probably this immersion in the hard realities of life that gives ancient Greek literature some of its special characteristics. Its firm hold on sanity and common sense for instance; its avoidance of sentimentality and paradox and various seductive kinds of folly ... Euripides has two long descriptions of battles ... and it is curious to compare these, the writings of the poet who had fought in a score of hand to hand battles, with the far more vivid rhapsodies of modern writers who have never so much as seen a man pointing a gun at them ...[1]

So, eschewing the 'seductive folly' of violent description, we just remind ourselves of what the four women and one man, 'standing out from the crowd who stood at a distance', were witnessing close-up – a young man in the prime of life dying publicly, naked under the noonday sun, scourged and fastened in a twisted position onto a crude wooden framework. The artists of the late Middle Ages may not have known what actually happened at a crucifixion, and they tended to sensationalism in their piety. Thus the typical crucifix, with the figure hanging straight down from nailed hands, has become part of our image of Christ.

That is certainly wrong. In such a position the victim would have died of suffocation comparatively quickly. But the Romans were real sadists; and we now have archaeological evidence to show the care they took both to produce and to prolong the agony of their victims, by partially supporting the weight of the body with the legs bent one over the other. Crucified slaves sometimes took days, not hours, to die; and we remember that in the case of Jesus, Pilate marvelled that he died so quickly, nonchalantly forgetting perhaps that he had first had him flogged to within an inch of his life, and not knowing either of the additional weight and burden of the sin of the world or of the deliberate giving up of his life, which Jesus achieved.

On the cross Jesus was completely victim, completely abandoned to all that spite and the laws of nature could do to him; but he was also completely in control, reigning as King from the awful tree, disposing of his own destiny as well as of the fate of the world. 'I lay down my life in order to take it up again. No one takes it from me' (John 10:17–18).

So Jesus, retaining self-control, also retains self-consciousness; and he sees his mother. Mary appears only twice in St John's Gospel – at the beginning, at Cana in Galilee, and at the end, at Calvary. Yet her presence at these two turning points is so powerful that she appears to inhabit the whole story. William Temple in his *Readings in St John's Gospel* comments that he knew the prophesy of Simeon, 'A sword shall pierce through thy own heart also' (Luke 2:35 AV/KJV), and would not have his mother witness his approaching dereliction, agony and end.

If, as tradition has it, Mary was by this time a widow, Jesus as her oldest son would be responsible for her welfare. So here we have a remarkable example of Jesus, having loved his own, loving them to the end and that not simply as an emotion, but by practical service and by fulfilling family obligations in accordance with the spirit and letter of the law of Moses. No word was further from his lips than 'Corban' (Mark 7:11); rather, 'Let it be so now; for it is proper for us in this way to fulfill all righteousness' (Matthew 3:15).

Jesus sees his beloved disciple also – the two people he loves most on earth comprehended in a single glance and undivided vision. The time has come for Jesus, while still taking care for the special earthly individual relationships which have been the essence of his incarnate life, to transcend them. So, in a word which recalls the first establishment of his supernatural authority at the wedding in Cana of Galilee, he calls Mary not 'mother' but 'woman' – the normal respectful form of address: 'Woman, here is your son.' Then he says to the disciple, 'Here is your mother,' in mutual commendation, establishing a relationship with simple words, which recall contemporary formulas of adoption.

This is part of a pattern which we see in the life and teaching of Jesus, in which that which is natural comes first, and then that which is spiritual. The natural is essential, and true religion never wholly parts company with it; but the natural is not all. Like Euripides, the Christian is not satisfied with bare realism. He has to go further and engage with other areas of the brain and regions of the mind, if he is to be fulfilled.

Family relationships are immensely important, and the discoveries and teachings of the great psychologists all reinforce just how important they are; but they are not the only relationships. The relationship of child to mother and father must in any case at some stage cease to be exclusive and all-embracing. Orphans and others require alternative relationships, and where primary relationships with parents have been seriously spoilt, the children may need to be released, even saved, from them. The salvation which Jesus brings avails not only for the sadism which took institutional form in the Roman Empire, but also for the myriads of little lives of ordinary people strangled in the tentacles of their families.

During his ministry Jesus had broken the bonds of the Middle Eastern natural family by stating that anyone who did the will of his heavenly Father was brother, sister and mother to him (Mark 3:35); but he retained the loyalty and affection and love of his mother and siblings, who were at the heart of the primitive church: 'All these were constantly devoting themselves to prayer, together with certain women, including Mary the mother of Jesus, as well as his brothers' (Acts 1:14). Doubtless Mary remembered, even as the sword pierced her heart, that as an adolescent Jesus had asserted his independence, not in revolt against his parents but in obedience to his heavenly calling: 'Did you not know that I must be in my Father's house?' (Luke 2:49).

If some of Jesus' sayings about the family seem harsh, we should remember that, having left the hearth at Nazareth with its given relationships, he found an alternative family by choice and by what Goethe would later call *Wahlverwandschaft*, 'elective affinity', with Lazarus and Mary and Martha, whom he loved, at Bethany. It is the example of Jesus and the victory won by him on the cross that makes the Christian heir to the possibilities of an immense richness and variety of warm, intimate and affectionate but proper relationships. As he said, 'There is no one who has left house or brothers or sisters or mother or father or children or fields, for my sake and for the sake of the good news, who will not receive a hundredfold now in this age – houses, brothers and sisters, mothers and children, and fields, with persecutions – and in the age to come eternal life' (Mark 10:29–30).

'Woman, here is your son', he says to Mary, not of her natural son but of the beloved disciple; and to him, 'Here is your mother', setting before them and us the image of the new spiritual relationships which are to characterise the church, different from but recognisable and describable in terms taken from natural relationships. Suddenly, compared with the claustrophobic narrowness of tribal or village life, personal relationships blossom under the new covenant in an infinite number of combinations such as we are still discovering. They have their own disciplines and renunciations; and the incest taboo between next of kin, which is universal in the natural family, is transferred intact to the extended family which is the church.

So we find St Paul telling the young bishop Timothy to treat an older man like a father, younger men as brothers, older women as mothers, younger women as sisters – 'with absolute purity' (1 Timothy 5:1–2). Once this principle is accepted, limitless personal resources are available for the blessing and healing of wounded souls. These things are possible when the natural is not suppressed or denied, but offered, taken with thanksgiving, broken and given for many, like the life and loves of Jesus, son of Mary and son of the Father.

5. MY GOD, MY GOD, WHY HAVE YOU FORSAKEN ME?

From noon on, darkness came over the whole land until three in the afternoon. And about three o'clock Jesus cried with a loud voice, 'Eli, Eli, lema sabachthani?' that is, 'My God, my God, why have you forsaken me?' When some of the bystanders heard it, they said, 'This man is calling for Elijah.' At once one of them ran and got a sponge, filled it with sour wine, put it on a stick, and gave it to him to drink. But the others said, 'Wait, let us see whether Elijah will come to save him.' (Matthew 27:45–49)

The beloved disciple goes away with Mary, and if he was indeed the source of the Fourth Gospel, that might explain why in his account he omits this saying, the most harrowing of all the words from the cross. It is as if the little light of human contact goes out with them and darkness covers the whole land, nature itself in awful harmony with the drama, which is being played out below (Matthew 27:45; Mark 15:33; Luke 23:44).

What was the nature of that darkness? It could not have been an eclipse, which cannot occur at the time of the Paschal full moon; it may have been a dust storm from the desert, which would have added to the victims' agony and intensified their thirst; it may have been thick clouds, heavy not only with rain but also with reference to the presence and power of God Almighty, El Shaddai, the Shekinah overshadowing all things both in nature and in history.

But whatever the physical effects, the meaning and intention of the Evangelists is clear: this is the darkness of sin, the shadow cast by the primordial fault in human nature which we call the fall, the gloom of all that separates humanity from the God who is life and light and love, what Milton called 'darkness visible'. And surely there is also a reference here to that 'dense darkness in all the land' (Exodus 10:22) which was the last but one of the ten plagues of Egypt, immediately before the death of the firstborn. Only this time, though the stage lighting is the same, the plot is different. Far from taking the firstborn of those who persecute and oppress his people Israel, God now gives his own firstborn Son for all.

At the ninth hour, when the end is near, Jesus cries out 'with a loud voice'; this is not that final loud cry of triumph, for which he needed to have his lips moistened; this is a cry from the very depths. Almost certainly he spoke, as St Matthew partially records it, in classical Hebrew, "Eli, Eli," quoting Psalm 22 as he would have learnt it twenty years ago in the synagogue from the village rabbi at Nazareth and from the domestic piety of Mary and Joseph. Mark, knowing that Jesus habitually spoke Aramaic, uses the form 'Eloi, Eloi'; but that is less likely to have been misheard as an appeal to Elijah.

I find it wholly credible and deeply moving that, with his mental as well as physical strength ebbing, doubtless with bouts of intermittent unconsciousness, overwhelmed by recurring waves of pain and anxiety and dread, in all this Jesus should have quoted something which is both poetry and prayer, taken from his own infancy and the infancy of his nation's culture and religion, as any one of us might, if God were merciful and we had been so brought up, babble on our deathbeds not only of green fields, but also in quotations from Shakespeare and from the Book of Common Prayer.

But what did Jesus mean by quoting 'Eli, Eli, lema sabachthani?' The Evangelists translate 'My God, my God, why have you forsaken me?' Are we to believe that Jesus was forsaken by God, indeed that God forsakes anyone? Or that he felt forsaken but that his feelings were not a true indication of his status? Or that he quoted the first verse of Psalm 22, which was all he could manage, in order to show his intention of praying the whole psalm with its triumphant conclusion, just as we might say 'Magnificat' or 'Nunc Dimittis' and mean the whole canticle, not just its first words? There is no possible way in which we can choose between these interpretations, and indeed the fulness of Christian meditation upon this cry requires that we maintain the richest possible range of meanings, for these words, in the circumstances in which they were spoken, have meant so much and such differing things to so many.

Probably the Evangelists, who with all the early church saw the cross as victory, meant the words to be taken as the opening of a prayer of profound faithfulness and trust in God by the unjustly persecuted – a prayer which is fully answered with total vindication:

> For he hath not despised, nor abhorred, the low estate of the poor:
> he hath not hid his face from him, but when he called unto
> him he heard him.
> My praise is of thee in the great congregation: my vows will I
> perform in the sight of them that fear him.

The poor shall eat and be satisfied: they that seek after the Lord
shall praise him; your heart shall live for ever.
All the ends of the world shall remember themselves, and be
turned unto the Lord: and all the kindreds of the nations shall
worship before him.
For the kingdom is the Lord's: and he is the Governor among the
people. (Psalm 22:24–31)

But that is to leap ahead with hindsight into the resurrection and the history of the spread of the gospel. Perhaps we should pause at the foot of the cross and note that the words as they stand are forlorn and desolate, and are most readily understood straight, as words of utter dereliction and despair. It may have been this which led Luke, in writing his Gospel for Gentiles less conversant with the Psalter, to omit these words entirely for fear of misunderstanding. Such misunderstanding is widespread in our culture and age, which spiritually and mentally and in much of its art is living in a wilderness of forsakenness and despair and in a permanent Holy Saturday after the crucifixion of hopes and before the resurrection to new life. So are all of us some of the time, and some of us all of the time. Art galleries and mental wards tell the same story; and so do inner cities and refugee camps and shanty towns and all places of human misery, destitution and neglect.

One reason for taking the quotation as it stands, in isolation from the rest of Psalm 22, is that it, and it alone, speaks directly to the heart of all those who in our age and in every age feel themselves, know themselves, to be utterly forsaken, lost and derelict, when isolation and the absence of every physical and mental comfort 'leaves the world to darkness and to me'.[2] It speaks as nothing else does to the tragedy and futility of human life, and it says 'Jesus has been here too'. When we say in the Creed, 'he descended into hell', we ought not to restrict the meaning and scope of that descent to the three days after his death. Many who live a living death know that it is even now that they are in hell. And just as the first interpretation speaks to those who can say with the psalmist, 'If I climb up into heaven, thou art there', so this interpretation speaks to those who say, 'and if I go down to hell, thou art there also' (Psalm 139:7).

Perhaps it was, as it has come to be called, dereliction. I believe it was. I believe that, mercifully and only for a while, Jesus, before he lost all consciousness, lost the consciousness, which had sustained him from infancy throughout his ministry, of the immediate presence and power of his heavenly Father; such was the weight and enormity of the sin of the world. To say 'lost' is not quite the right word; it implies too great passivity. Jesus willed actively to give it up, to take this upon himself, to be totally overwhelmed as man by the power of darkness, so that he had no human foreknowledge or certainty of the risen life, no assurance of anything but that he would die in torment.

The risk Jesus took of annihilation, his vulnerability to nothingness, was at that moment total. At that moment, the responsibility for maintaining the everlasting and unbroken relationship of love between the Father and the Son in the Godhead was carried, as it always is since eternity and before the creation of time, by the Holy and life-giving Spirit, who proceeds from the Father through the Son. Even in this dark hour, the Spirit bound Father and Son together in one unbroken fellowship of love – a love of which Jesus was now unaware.

For even the cry of total dereliction is addressed to God: where else? There is a kind of passionate atheism, a crying out to the God who is no longer an object of mental certainty, which is infinitely deeper and closer to God's heart, and to which, as he has shown in the resurrection of Jesus, he responds, more than to bloodless and genteel theism, the mere notional assent to propositions about his existence, or superficial protestations of affection and obedience. It is the difference between the attitudes of the prodigal son and those of his elder brother, the difference between the two sons in the vineyard and between the Pharisee and the tax collector (Luke 15:11–32; Matthew 21:28–32; Luke 18:9–14). As the German scholar Martin Dibelius said, 'The Jesus who quoted a word of the Bible in prayer had not lost faith in God.'[3]

Is it fanciful, I wonder, to see in Jesus' ability, even on the cross, to say 'My God' good news for nihilists, atheists and agnostics? This phrase is a pointer towards and warrant for the confession of faith of those who, like doubting Thomas, have experienced so deeply the crucifixion of their hopes that they are not taken in by easy and secondhand assurances but simply gaze upon his wounds and say, 'My Lord and my God!' (John 20:28).

6. I AM THIRSTY

> After this, when Jesus knew that all was now finished, he said (in order to fulfill the scripture), 'I am thirsty.' A jar full of sour wine was standing there. So they put a sponge full of the wine on a branch of hyssop and held it to his mouth. When Jesus had received the wine, he said 'It is finished.' Then he bowed his head and gave up his spirit. (John 19:28–29)

Even at the end, Jesus reigns; subject to the forces which he created and which are now crushing the life out of him, he causes them to bear his meaning and purposes. With all the quiet control which he has shown throughout his ministry, he knows that all is finished; but it is not enough that he should know it, it has to be proclaimed. The Word made flesh must, while he is yet in his flesh, utter the words of life. And for that he needs his parched mouth and throat moistened, so he says, 'I am thirsty.' This is the only reference in all the accounts of the crucifixion to pain or even discomfort, and its motive is not alleviation but proclamation.

John comments 'in order to fulfil the scripture'. This should not be taken as meaning that Jesus, like a well rehearsed actor, was simply speaking memorised lines written for him in the Hebrew Scriptures. 'So that' is much closer in meaning to 'and so'. Jesus said, 'I am thirsty', and so the Scriptures were fulfilled; and here John uses a strong and unusual word, again extending the meaning beyond the mere fulfilment of oracles. John sees the crucifixion as the fulfilment of the meaning of the Scriptures taken as a whole. In it their full import is enacted; the disparate stands are brought together; obscurities, like rough places, are made plain; and the whole is brought to a perfection, which, as a whole, is greater than the sum of its parts. The Hebrew Scriptures are of inestimable value. They are the finest thing the ancient world affords; but the crucifixion of the Word made flesh is their end, in the sense of their fulfilment, to those who believe that Jesus is the Messiah.

Yet the general is made specific in the particular, and John has especially in mind Psalm 69:21: 'for my thirst they gave me vinegar to drink'. This was part of the destiny of the Lord's Messiah, the Suffering Servant of God; and both in the original psalm and in Luke's account of the crucifixion, the offer of sour wine or vinegar is part of the mockery, an additional petty and spiteful humiliation.

> Thy rebuke hath broken my heart;
>> I am full of heaviness:
> I looked for some to have pity on me,
>> But there was no man,
>> Neither found I any to comfort me.

> *They gave me gall to eat:*
> *And when I was thirsty*
> *They gave me vinegar to drink. (Psalm 69:21–22)*

This, the psalmist says, is the fate of the just man who on earth does the will of God. And a simple, almost involuntary act of kindness by an anonymous Roman soldier with his homely sponge and hyssop becomes both the symbol of that fate and also the instrument of God's wider purpose, to declare his salvation in the sight of the nations (Psalm 98:2).

So Jesus thirsts and drinks; and each of these actions has its own deeper meaning. We tend to think of thirst either as passive, something that happens to us, or as an involuntary state: I am thirsty. But here it is an activity: 'I thirst'. In this and in all things, even at the end, Jesus does not cease to do the work with which the Father has entrusted him. He thirsts as they do, of whom he once said, 'Blessed are those who hunger and thirst for righteousness, for they will be filled' (Matthew 5:6). He thirsts as they do of whom the psalmist sings:

> *Like as the heart desireth the water brooks:*
> *so longeth my soul after thee, O God.*
> *My soul is athirst for God,*
> *Yea, even for the living God. (Psalm 42:1–2)*

Throughout his life and in his death, Jesus thirsted with these two great thirsts: the thirst for justice and the thirst for God. More than anything else the world needs men and women who will thirst this double thirst, even if, like Oscar Romero of El Salvador or Janani Luwum of Kampala, it kills them. Helder Camara, Mother Theresa, Desmond Tutu, the Prior of Taizé – wherever you see inspiring leadership in the Christian tradition, you see the thirst for God and the thirst for justice yoked together. And wherever one of these thirsts is thirsted on its own without the other, there is that imbalance which technically is called heresy, and which always leads to schism. Various kinds of political ideology and of utopianism thirst for justice, but lacking the thirst for God, they lead to new forms of oppression, futility and despair. Various kinds of cults and meditative techniques thirst for God, but lacking the thirst for righteousness, they turn in on themselves and, missing neighbour, they miss God too. It is not a simple matter for Jesus to say, 'I am thirsty.'

Having at the start refused the kindly offer of drugged wine in order that he might die actively, alert, with all his faculties intact, he now receives this vinegar and drinks. On several occasions he had spoken of the sufferings that lay ahead of him as a cup.

- He had asked the bold sons of Zebedee, who wanted to sit on his right hand and on his left in the Kingdom of Heaven, 'Are you able to drink the cup that I drink?' (Mark 10:38).
- On the night in which he was betrayed he took the cup after supper, saying, 'This cup that is poured out for you is the new covenant in my blood' (Luke 22:20), having first declared, 'I tell you that from now on I will not drink of the fruit of the vine until the kingdom of God comes' (Luke 22:18).
- In Gethsemane, where in an agony of prayer he took the decision to be obedient from which all the rest followed, he prayed, 'Abba, Father, for you all things are possible; remove this cup from me; yet, not what I want, but what you want' (Mark 14:36).
- And to the rash, impetuous Peter, seeking to defend him with a drawn sword in his hand, he said, 'Put your sword back into its sheath. Am I not to drink the cup that the Father has given me?' (John 18:11).

And for the persecuted Christians of the early church, the cup was not only a cup of rejoicing, a foretaste of the banquet in the kingdom of heaven. It was also a bitter cup, a cup of sorrow and of suffering.

Now the last dregs are drunk. Having loved his own, he loved them to the end; and it is this love to the uttermost which we commemorate, whenever in the Eucharist we obey his command and do this, as often as we drink it, in remembrance of him.

QUESTIONS

1. What was Jesus' attitude to families? And what is ours?

2. In what sense is Jesus' cry of dereliction 'good news for nihilists, atheists and agnostics'?

3. What is the closest you have come to dereliction?

4. Do you thirst both for God and for justice?

CHAPTER 11

Words from the Tree (3)

Fulfilment, Committal and Recognition

7. IT IS FINISHED

When Jesus had received the wine, he said, 'It is finished.' Then he bowed his head and gave up his spirit. (John 19:30)

The first three Gospels record that before he died, Jesus cried out a second time in a loud voice. John omits this detail, but he does tell us what he said. It is idle to speculate how he came to know, and, if he knew, why the others did not. Perhaps the beloved disciple had returned to his place by the cross and the crucified. Perhaps the actual word is his interpretation of the cry, in which case it is worth noting that his interpretation is not different from, but the same as, that of the other Evangelists.

That a man could cry out in a loud voice at all, after crucifixion, was an astonishing sign of power and self-affirmation. He is revealed as victor, not in spite of but because of, his cry. The last thing it is, is a cry of relief or of self-pity. It is a cry of victory, of triumph and of achievement, and it is as such that it is presented in the Gospels.

The usual English translation 'It is finished', with the hint of 'Now it's over', does not do this saying justice. Its full meaning is a mixture of 'it is completed, it is consummated, it is fulfilled, it is ended' – with the emphasis on the achievement of the end to which and for which it was designed. I like the German, *'Es ist vollbracht'*, especially as set by Johann Sebastian Bach. This word speaks of the total attainment of goals and objectives, but it leaves unexpressed exactly what those ends are. 'It is finished', cries Jesus, but he does not answer the question, 'What is finished?' In crucifixion as in resurrection, he leaves us to fill an emptiness with a faith like his in the loving purposes of the Father. Thus grace draws out faith, and Christ even on the cross involves his followers in the interpretation and development of his triumph.

The first thing the Evangelists intend their readers to see fulfilled is 'everything written about [the Messiah] in the law of Moses, the prophets, and the psalms' (Luke 24:44). This is done partly in details, such as the dicing for Jesus' possessions (Psalm 22:18) or the offer of vinegar to drink (Psalm 69:21); and John is going to point to the spear thrust as fulfilling the word 'when they look on the one whom they have pierced' (Zechariah 12:10; cp. Psalm 22:17), as well as to the non-breaking of his legs in fulfilment of the word, 'and you shall not break any of its bones' (Exodus 12:46).

This style of presentation does not necessarily speak directly to us, though it may. But it was just the way to present the astonishing facts of the crucifixion of Christ to men and women of the first century. We always have difficulty in communicating something absolutely new and unique; it can only be conveyed in terms of the old and familiar, in this case by quotation from the Hebrew Scriptures, from Israel's literary and historical and religious heritage.

In a wider sense, God's victory in Christ on the cross is offered as the fulfilment of the hopes of all humankind, beginning with the hope of Israel for *shalom*, for peace with righteousness and justice – not a mere absence of war but a positive state of well-being for man and beast in and with nature, in which 'the wolf shall live with the lamb, the leopard shall lie down with the kid, the calf and the lion and the fatling together, and a little child shall lead them' (Isaiah 11:6), and 'they shall beat their swords into plowshares, and their spears into pruning hooks; nation shall not lift up sword against nation, neither shall they learn war any more; but they shall all sit under their own vines and under their own fig trees, and no one shall make them afraid' (Micah 4:3–4; see also Isaiah 2:2–4). This hope of Israel is a broad-hearted magnanimous hope for all, and its fulfilment begins when 'it is finished' on the cross.

The prophets saw that our best hopes cannot be fulfilled in the world as it is; the new life will require a new heaven and a new earth, so the accent in all the most profound prophesies is on transformation, change and newness, on the old world travailing to give birth to a new one. In the New Testament, too, the sufferings of Jesus on the cross are seen as birth pangs, the birth pangs of a new humanity. Jesus himself had foretold his sufferings in these terms: 'When a woman is in labor, she has pain, because her hour has come. But when her child is born, she no longer remembers the anguish because of the joy of having brought a human being into the world' (John 16:21). So runs the current translation, but it conceals a profound pun. The last phrase could also be translated, 'for joy that humankind is born into the cosmos'. Paul consistently talks of the achievement of Christ as the bringing to birth of a new humanity. By his life, Jesus lived a truly human life; and by his death, he makes it possible for others, for the first time, also to live a truly human life like his.

He had not only fulfilled the expectations of men and women. Much more than that, he had fulfilled the expectations of God. As he himself said, 'I glorified you on earth by finishing the work that you gave me to do' (John 17:4). Jesus did not only live a life; he exercised a ministry and completed a task. He first went about doing good, and then he went up to Jerusalem to draw upon himself the power of evil vested in Jewish and Gentile political and religious institutions, as well as in particular individuals. Of course, his Passion must be described in terms of passivity, of Jesus learning obedience through the things he suffers, the things that happen to him (Hebrews 5:8). But it must also be understood as a work, as something which he does, as an outworking in particular circumstances of the divine energy and of divine power.

Enduring, hanging on, keeping going, is worthwhile work; there are many human situations of stress or confrontation or harassment or provocation where that is the case. Hard physical work can be a relief from mental and spiritual endurance; and the work of healing the brokenhearted and the broken-spirited always has this as a vital component. So does the work, to which all of us some day should turn our hands, of holy dying, of dying as a positive act and achievement, extinguished but undefeated, like Jesus. On the cross it is the power of sin and death and hell which is broken and defeated, not the spirit of God and man in Jesus. 'I was dead, and see, I am alive forever and ever; and I have the keys of [that is, power over] Death and of Hades' (Revelation 1:18).

Jesus gave a loud cry and said, 'It is finished.' For the Word of God, the agent of creation, finishing things is his typical activity, finishing a creation which can be seen as good but not yet perfect, finishing tables and chairs and ploughs and carts in the Nazareth workshop of Joseph and Son, making yokes that fit easily so that burdens are light, finishing the work which his Father has given him to do, the agent of our salvation and the example of what we might become in him, the 'pioneer and perfecter of our faith' (Hebrews 12:2).

The writer of the letter to the Hebrews sums it up for us:

> In the days of his flesh, Jesus offered up prayers and supplications, with loud cries and tears, to the one who was able to save him from death, and he was heard because of his reverent submission. Although he was a Son, he learned obedience through what he suffered; and having been made perfect, he became the source of eternal salvation for all who obey him ... (Hebrews 5:7–9)

8. FATHER, INTO YOUR HANDS I COMMEND MY SPIRIT

> Then Jesus ... said, 'Father, into your hands I commend my spirit.' Having said this, he breathed his last. (Luke 23:46)

John continues: 'Then he bowed his head and gave up his spirit'. Although he alone of the Evangelists records the bowing of the head, he adds no words. For him, 'it is finished' is the end, it is the glory of the cross, nothing verbal can be added to it; but the word is completed and prolonged by an action, as a greeting might be by a kiss or handshake, or a farewell by a bow or wave. He bowed his head.

This is an action, positively willed by Jesus himself as his last act on earth. John does not say that 'his head fell forward' or 'he collapsed', any more than any of the Evangelists ever simply says, 'he died', or implies that his life was taken from him. The life of Jesus was not stolen from an unsuspecting or helpless victim. On the contrary, he gave it, of his own volition; he bowed his head and gave up his spirit (John 19:30).

But to whom did he give it? To the centurion and the four Roman soldiers who were the agents of his crucifixion? To the scribes and chief priests, the Sanhedrin and the high priest? To Herod and Pontius Pilate? To the crowd, both of Jews and, as Acts records, of people from every nation under heaven? To you and me? No, not exactly. He gave up his life *for* us and *for* all men and women everywhere; but, more than that, he gave it up *to* the Father, bowing his head with limitless trust and affection and in humble and grateful adoration. The last action of Jesus on earth is meek and pious, intimate though public, and deeply human, a symbol of all that is best in and most typical of humankind, a worshipful and thankful, you might almost say eucharistic, attitude towards the God and Father of all.

Our Victorian forebears used to enjoy collecting famous last words, whether edifying or amusing, perhaps on the assumption that there is something especially significant about the last in a series, something that finally reveals the nature of the series as a whole. My favourite last words, because to my mind they so exactly disclose a lifetime of discipleship, of following Jesus to the end, are those of John Chrysostom – exiled, harried by enemies in the church and at court, ill and exhausted and dying in a ditch beside the Byzantium road: 'Thank God for everything.' And just as the Patriarch of Constantinople, at the last, was shown to be what he had always been, a grateful disciple, so Jesus at the last is seen to be essentially and eternally a son. 'Father', he says quietly, 'into your hands I commend my spirit.'

The word 'commend' (or in some translations 'commit') was a word in common use for depositing something valuable with a friend or relative. That is Jesus' attitude to his life; it is both something precious and something that can be given up. This choice of word is one of the points where we can see that, for all the voluntariness of the death of Christ as self-oblation in a consciously willed act, it is as far from suicide as it is from accident. There is no false pathos, nothing world-weary or life-denying about this death. It is a true offering, and a pattern of all offering, because the life that is given up is loved and cherished and appreciated, as only a gift from a beloved father can be.

King David had said, when insisting on paying for the site of the temple, 'I will not offer [sacrifices] to the LORD my God that cost me nothing' (2 Samuel 24:24). When his time comes, Jesus, great David's greater Son, who is himself the temple of the Holy Spirit, the tabernacle or dwelling place of God on earth, offers only that which has cost him everything, even life itself.

We remember the prototype of this sacrifice. In Genesis 22 Abraham takes his only son, Isaac, through whom alone, he believes, God's will for humankind can be achieved. In obedience he prepares to offer him on Mount Moriah. The story is told from Abraham's point of view, because it is the story of the testing of his faith. But Isaac must have had a point of view too, and his only recorded utterance begins with the words 'my father'. The story implies both devotion and obedience, with the awful irony that Isaac's trust is misplaced. There is something dream-like about the way he accompanies Abraham, trusting but half-suspecting; and part of the moral of the story is that he who is to be absolutely trusted is God alone.

In response to the teaching of the prophets the ancient Hebrews invented a wholly new way of telling stories whereby the chief characters are not heroes in the usual sense of the word. God above is the only true hero; men and women are set free from the demands of heroism in a literary sense to live credible human lives, which are a mixture of good and evil, light and darkness, insight and, as in the case of Abraham believing that God requires human sacrifice, appalling blindness. But because Isaac has been truly offered, because the disposition of his and Abraham's heart is right, God acts to make his abundant blessings available to their descendants 'as numerous as the stars of heaven and as the sand that is on the seashore' (Genesis 22:17), and through them to all the nations of the earth. This story marks the beginning of the end of human sacrifice. Not for nothing does Benjamin Britten interweave it with the traditional words of the Mass and of Wilfred Owen's poetry in his 'War Requiem'.

Jesus commits his spirit to the Father, and the word for 'spirit' is rightly taken here basically to mean his human life. That is the gift, which he is entrusting to the Father's keeping. But there is an additional meaning, for it is the same word as is used for the Holy Spirit. Jesus had described his death with the words 'I am going to the Father', and to the amazement of his disciples he had said that it was expedient that he should go away (John 16:17). The Father would send them another Comforter, even the Spirit of truth, who would be with them forever (John 14:16).

The story of the fulfilment of that promise is told in different ways. Luke tells of a dramatic and public outpouring of the Spirit at Pentecost; John of a more intimate gift to the disciples behind locked doors on Easter Day. But John prepares for this by showing how, at the very moment of his going away, Jesus, as it were, makes the Spirit, which is also his spirit, available, even if its availability is not taken up until disciples respond with faith in the resurrection.

In every respect and to the last detail – in public life, in personal intimacy and in the innermost life of the Godhead – the Son has indeed done all. There is nothing that should be done which has been left undone. The Word of God, who is the agent of creation, doing all things well, as the agent of our redemption and the initiator of our sanctification, does all things equally well. And Peter, in his first letter to the early Christians, sums up for us the implications of Jesus' seventh and last word from the cross, 'Father, into your hands I commend my spirit,' when he says, 'Therefore, let those suffering in accordance with God's will entrust themselves to a faithful Creator, while continuing to do good' (1 Peter 4:19).

9. TRULY THIS WAS GOD'S SON

Then Jesus cried again with a loud voice and breathed his last. At that moment the curtain of the temple was torn in two, from top to bottom. The earth shook, and the rocks were split. The tombs also were opened, and many bodies of the saints who had fallen asleep were raised. After his resurrection they came out of the tombs and entered the holy city and appeared to many. Now when the centurion and those with him, who were keeping watch over Jesus, saw the earthquake and what took place, they were terrified and said, 'Truly this man was God's Son!'

Many women were also there, looking on from a distance; they had followed Jesus from Galilee and had provided for him. Among them were Mary Magdalene, and Mary the mother of James and Joseph, and the mother of the sons of Zebedee. (Matthew 27:50–56)

The mood changes completely. After the affectionate intimacy of Father, Son and Spirit, suddenly all is public and dramatic again. There has already been darkness. Now there is an earthquake and apparitions, the rending of the veil and the centurion's confession. In Matthew's narrative all these things, like the extraordinary occurrences surrounding the birth of Jesus, indicate that the death of Jesus too is an act of God – of God in man, it is true, but also of God in nature, in history, and in the public life of church and state. These things were not done in a corner; they were displayed for all to see and for all to respond to.

This is Matthew's pictorial and narrative way of saying something, which Paul sets out more systematically in his letters, namely, that the death of Christ is the definitive event among all events, and that its effects reverberate not only throughout the lives of men and women, Jew and Gentile, but also through the very fabric of Jewish religion and Roman polity, through life and death and through the foundations of the world itself, through geography and history, through space and time. There is nothing in heaven or on earth, nothing in all creation, which is not radically transformed by the death of Christ. It is an event of what we would now call 'cosmic significance' and it is at the heart of the preaching of Peter and Paul and of the whole primitive church.

The 'saints' whom Matthew evokes here would be the great Jewish heroes of faith, of whom the writer of the letter to the Hebrews speaks, starting with the righteous Abel, the son of Adam, going on to Enoch and Noah and pausing to retell the story of Abraham and Isaac.

> By faith Abraham, when put to the test, offered up Isaac. He who had received the promises was ready to offer up his only son, of whom he had been told, 'It is through Isaac that descendants shall be named for you'. He considered the fact that God is able even to raise someone from the dead – and figuratively speaking, he did receive him back. (Hebrews 11:17–19)

Here we see how the early Christian experience of the resurrection of Jesus from the dead transforms the way a Jewish person read the Hebrew Scriptures, and how easily a writer could move between speaking figuratively and apparently straightforward narrative.

The list in Hebrews goes on through Isaac, Jacob and Joseph, pausing again at Moses and then hurrying on through Rahab the harlot, Gideon, Barak, Samson, Jephthah, David, Samuel and the prophets, relating all that they achieved through faith, 'the assurance of things hoped for, the conviction of things not seen' (Hebrews 11:1). In particular it recounts the way the righteous were tortured, mocked, scourged and imprisoned, stoned, sawn asunder, killed with the sword, 'destitute, persecuted, tormented – of whom the world was not worthy' (Hebrews 11:37–38). Then the writer goes on to show the same motive as Matthew for invoking the saints of old: 'Yet all these, though they were commended for their faith, did not receive what was promised, since God had provided something better so that they would not, *apart from us*, be made perfect' (Hebrews 11:39–40, italics added).

Picture Matthew's scenario: Jesus dead upon the cross, the earth quaking and the rocks rending, the tombs opened, and many bodies of the saints that had fallen asleep were raised; 'after his resurrection they came out of the tombs and entered the holy city and appeared to many' (Matthew 27:51–53). Clearly they are put into the picture to be witnesses, both to the enduring value of faithfulness and also to the power of God to raise from the dead. But they are invoked *for us*. So the writer of the letter to the Hebrews goes on:

> Therefore, since we are surrounded by so great a cloud of witnesses, let us also lay aside every weight and the sin that clings so closely, and let us run with perseverance the race that is set before us, looking to Jesus the pioneer and perfecter of our faith, who for the sake of the joy that was set before him endured the cross, disregarding its shame, and has taken his seat at the right hand of the throne of God. (Hebrews 12:1–2)

Beside these details, which only Matthew records, are two other witnesses, whom Mark and Luke also regard as highly significant, the veil and the voice, the first especially significant for Jews, the second for Gentiles.

The veil, or rather veils – for there were two enormous curtains right across the width of the building – were an essential part of the temple, dividing the Holy Place, where the daily services took place, from the Holy of Holies, where only the high priest went once a year on the Day of Atonement, *Yom Kippur*. The strength and weakness of the religion of the old covenant was that it stressed separation, the separation of clean and unclean, the separation of Jew and Gentile and, above all, the separation of humankind and God, which could only be temporarily overcome by the fulfilment of the law regarding sacrifices. The rending of the veil symbolises the opening up of direct access to the inner presence of God through the death of Jesus, the perfect sacrifice, the sacrifice to end all sacrifices.

It is this insight above all which has formed the church's understanding of the Eucharist or Holy Communion as a sacrifice and means of access to the Father through the Son (Hebrews 10:19–22). Within a generation of the crucifixion the temple was destroyed by the Romans and the whole sacrificial system dismantled, so early Christian interpretations also see the rending of the veil, like the rending of garments, as a sign of mourning: the temple grieving for her own destruction. It is difficult for us fully to comprehend what it must have meant to the Jews, though we may get a glimpse when we see them praying today at the Wailing Wall. For Paul, however, the chief effect of the death of Christ is the overcoming of the separation between Jew and Gentile. It is a theme to which he returns time and time again, notably in his letter to the Ephesians, where he says:

For he is our peace; in his flesh he has made both groups into one and has broken down the dividing wall, that is, the hostility between us. He has abolished the law with its commandments and ordinances, that he might create in himself one new humanity in place of the two, thus making peace, and might reconcile both groups to God in one body through the cross, thus putting to death that hostility through it. (Ephesians 2:14–16)

For Paul the miracle is that in Christ Jesus the Gentiles who were far off have now been brought near through the blood of Christ (Ephesians 2:13). And of this, at the foot of the cross, at the very moment of the death of Christ, the centurion is the first fruit and example. Even before Pentecost and the outpouring of the Spirit upon all flesh, a Gentile is converted to belief by the power of the cross of Christ alone. Mark, whose account is the earliest, rightly stresses this point. 'Now when the centurion, who stood facing him, saw that in this way he breathed his last, he said, "Truly this man was God's Son!"' (Mark 15:39). It is no wonder that Paul, the great apostle to the Gentiles, resolved to preach nothing but Christ and him crucified. No wonder that throughout two millennia of the expansion of Christianity into all the world, it can truthfully be said of all effective apostles and missionaries: 'preaching but the cross of shame, rebel hearts for Christ ye tame'.[1]

The earthquake, the apparitions and the rending of the veil are scenery; they fade into the background when human speech holds the centre of the stage. In the story of Elijah, it was said,

Now there was a great wind, so strong that it was splitting mountains and breaking rocks in pieces before the LORD, but the LORD was not in the wind; and after the wind an earthquake, but the LORD was not in the earthquake; and after the earthquake a fire, but the LORD was not in the fire; and after the fire a sound of sheer silence. When Elijah heard it, he wrapped his face in his mantle and went out and stood at the entrance of the cave. Then there came a voice to him [in the traditional translation 'a still small voice'] ... (1 Kings 19:11–13)

Similarly Matthew, after all the stupendous audio visual effects in his crucifixion story, ends the drama with a still small voice: 'Truly this was God's Son.'

POSTSCRIPT

There is a curious and deeply moving contemporary echo of this confession, perhaps closer to its Lukan form, 'Certainly, this man was innocent' (Luke 23:47). An SS doctor in Hitler's Third Reich (with the rank of captain, which is roughly equivalent to centurion) witnessed the execution of Dietrich Bonhoeffer on 9 April 1945, not knowing who the prisoner was. Later he wrote:

> Through the half open door ... I saw Pastor Bonhoeffer ... kneeling on the floor praying devoutly to his God. I was most deeply moved by the way this lovable man prayed, so devout and so certain that God heard his prayer. At the place of execution he again said a short prayer and then climbed the steps to the gallows, brave and composed. In the almost fifty years I have worked as a doctor I have hardly ever seen a man die so entirely submissive to the will of God.[2]

QUESTIONS

1. Jesus said, 'It is finished.' What is there left for us to do?

2. What are the implications of regarding the death of Jesus upon the cross as a sacrifice?

3. Why is the cross at the centre of our faith and witness?

CHAPTER 12

The Tree of Life

Resurrection and Restoration

THE GARDEN OF RESURRECTION

But Mary stood weeping outside the tomb. As she wept, she bent over to look into the tomb; and she saw two angels in white, sitting where the body of Jesus had been lying, one at the head and the other at the feet. They said to her, 'Woman, why are you weeping?' She said to them, 'They have taken away my Lord, and I do not know where they have laid him.' When she had said this, she turned around and saw Jesus standing there, but she did not know that it was Jesus. Jesus said to her, 'Woman, why are you weeping? Whom are you looking for?' Supposing him to be the gardener, she said to him, 'Sir, if you have carried him away, tell me where you have laid him, and I will take him away.' Jesus said to her, 'Mary!' She turned and said to him in Hebrew, 'Rabbouni!' (which means Teacher). Jesus said to her, 'Do not hold on to me, because I have not yet ascended to the Father. But go to my brothers and say to them, "I am ascending to my Father and your Father, to my God and your God."' Mary Magdalene went and announced to the disciples, 'I have seen the Lord'; and she told them that he had said these things to her. (John 20:11 – 18)

For centuries the Christian imagination has fed itself on a romantic and even salacious picture of Mary Magdalene, a remarkable woman, styled by the Eastern Orthodox Church the equal of the apostles. That picture is based on an identification of Mary of Magdala, the witness to the resurrection and one of a group of female companions of Jesus and the Twelve, with the woman who was a sinner in the house of Simon the Leper, with Mary of Bethany and even with the woman taken in adultery, not to mention more recent fantasies, both mediaeval and modern. None of these is proved and indeed none of them is even probable. So Mary may stand first as patron saint of those who suffer by having a public image projected upon them, which does not correspond to their own reality nor help their own needs, but which can destroy image and image maker alike.

The only credible evidence about Mary comes from Luke 8:2–3, which names three of the many women who supported Jesus and the apostles on their mission and 'who provided for them out of their resources'. One of them was 'Mary, called Magdalene, from whom seven demons had gone out'. This almost certainly means that she was a woman with what used to be called a hysterical type of personality, whose rapid swings of mood and clinging nature men found difficult to cope with and therefore ascribed to demons. Of course simply labelling the condition in an analytical and objective way 'hysterical', or better still 'mixed hysterical and schizoid', may just be a modern equivalent of talking about demons – a way of keeping both the problem and the person at a distance.

Labelling may be a necessary stage on the journey to help and healing; the important thing for us to realise is that Jesus went the second mile and the whole way. Just by being himself, the one who uniquely can say 'I am' and it suffices, he filled the gaps in her personality, piecing the fragments together and producing order out of chaos. As St Luke says, he 'cured [her] of evil spirits and in-firmities', because uniquely with him her inner chaos was not re-flected in the distorting mirror of another inner chaos. In him she could now be herself, an undistorted image, part of a fellowship; she could lead a useful and fulfilled life and enjoy the company of the other women, of the apostles and of Jesus himself. With Jesus she had a personality to contribute to the common wealth of fel-lowship. So far so good – so long as she was with Jesus and Jesus with her.

But she was also one of the women who witnessed the cruci-fixion, a disaster as it seemed for all concerned, except perhaps for Barabbas. The death of Jesus on the cross was, however, uniquely catastrophic for Mary of Magdala. The Blessed Virgin Mary had lost a son, Mary of Bethany a companion, Peter a leader and John a man who loved him. Besides all these things Mary had lost the mainstay of her own personality, for that is what he was to her. Mary his mother had John to look after her and Mary of Bethany had Martha and Lazarus. Without Jesus, Peter was bereaved and remorseful but still very much himself, with his own means of coping with emotion, the company of other men, competitive sport (even racing John to the tomb), exercising leadership, going fishing. None of these things was available to Mary of Magdala.

Without Jesus, Mary was empty; the personality which he had put together from seven shards was shattered again; the pitcher was broken at the well and everything was poured out. So she stands outside the sepulchre weeping; that is all she can do. She is so alienated and distracted that she can only meet the resurrec-tion with bewilderment. On her lips, 'They have taken away my Lord, and I do not know where they have laid him' means, 'They have dismembered me, taken me apart from myself, and I do not know where or what I am.' Even when she looks at Jesus and he speaks to her, she is so overwhelmed with grief that she does not recognise him.

So Mary is also the patron saint of those who, while they are drowning in their own misery, cannot see what they are looking at. As Bishop Westcott comments, 'She was preoccupied with her own reflections. We see that only which we have the inward power of seeing. Till Mary was placed in something of spiritual harmony with the Lord she could not recognise him'. Instead she distracts herself, as we might do, by volunteering to do the impossible and carry the dead body away on her own back, when he is offering her precisely what Westcott calls 'spiritual harmony with the Lord'.[1]

He puts two questions to Mary: 'Why are you weeping?' and 'Whom are you looking for?' – two questions which in their depth and simplicity and universality of application correspond in the New Testament to the two questions with which, in the Hebrew Scriptures, God the Father, when he comes seeking the first man and woman in the garden, opens his never-ending conversation with humankind: '[Adam,] where are you?' and 'Who told you that you were naked?' Like his Father, Jesus puts questions in the garden not because he needs to know the answer but because Mary does. She needs to recognise in this manner of questioning her teacher – *Rabbouni* – as she does when he gives her her name, and her life and her soul, and restores the old relationship. Only the old relationship is now a new relationship.

Once Mary has been put back together again, she can be dissuaded from clinging to him like the lover in the Song of Solomon. She can be given a task ('go to my brothers and say to them'); she can be helped to move from being *with* Christ to being *in* Christ, to replacing the old intimacy of physical presence with a new fellowship in the Spirit and in the sacrament of his body and blood.

The old relationship restored is a new relationship; and the power by which that is achieved is the power by which God raised

Jesus Christ from the dead, the power which St Paul in his letters equates with the power whereby God created the world (2 Corinthians 5:17), the power of love which is stronger not only than death but also than dissolution and decay. He is speaking of the transformation of his own life by the Spirit of the risen Christ when he says, 'even though we once knew Christ from a human point of view, we know him no longer in that way' (2 Corinthians 5:16) – but how perfectly this sentence fits Mary Magdalene's experience. He goes on, 'so if anyone is in Christ, there is a new creation'. Then the conclusion follows logically: 'everything old has passed away; see, everything has become new!'

Why did the risen Christ appear first to Mary of Magdala, rather than to Mary his mother or to Peter or to John? There are two answers to this question. He appeared to her first because she needed him most. In a curious way this first act of the risen Christ in the garden mirrors the last act of the dying Christ upon the cross, when working his great work of saving the whole world he still found time to love his neighbour, the man who was actually next to him, the penitent thief upon his cross who needed him in that instant, not later, and who received the promise, 'This day you will be with me in paradise – in a cool enclosed garden like Eden at the dawn of creation.' And now three days later Mary of Magdala is with him in a cool enclosed garden at the dawn of the new creation, and Paradise is regained.

To the Good Shepherd who goes after the one lost lamb in order that the flock may be complete, to the Father for whom no sparrow falls to the ground unheeded, to the Creator who caused galaxies to wax and wane so that you and I might live, the restoration of a single broken human personality is an act of love, equivalent to creating the universe in the first place by the same pattern of activity in bringing order out of chaos. That is the scope of resurrection. As Jesus prophesied, after the anguish and travail of the birth pangs of a new world, humankind at last is born into the cosmos, the universe changes course and, in the terminology of Teilhard de Chardin in *The Phenomenon of Man*, the divergence from alpha turns into convergence upon omega. At that same instant it becomes real, local, personal in Mary of Magdala, his neighbour, the woman who is actually next to him and who needs him in this moment – now, not later.

The Christ who rises to be crowned King of the universe does not appear in the first instant to Pilate or to Caiaphas or to any of the mighty upon earth; there is no room for the risen Christ in those who are full of themselves. He rises to the brokenhearted, to the poor in spirit, to the meek and lowly, filling the empty with good things, giving them the faith to see, the faith to know, the faith to follow him in his risen life. St Paul knew this and put it into words when he wrote to the Corinthians. Mary of Magdala knew it. She ran and told the disciples; and the rest, as they say, is history – not history BC but history AD.

So, thirdly, Mary is the patron saint of those who hear the word of God and keep it – not keep it to themselves, but share it out from a full heart and bring forth fruit, thirtyfold, sixtyfold, even hundredfold. And that is the second reason why the risen Jesus appeared first to her, because of all the disciples she was, by her constancy and newfound strength of character, the one most suited to be the herald of the resurrection – and the apostle to the apostles. We may be glad that that little band of disciples was not in a position to take literally Paul's later words to the Corinthians that women should keep silence in the church (1 Corinthians 14:34); for then neither they nor we would so much as have heard of the resurrection of our Lord Jesus Christ, that great Shepherd of the sheep, whom the God of peace brought again from the dead through the blood of the everlasting covenant, to make us perfect in every good work to do his will (see Hebrews 13:20).

THE GARDEN CITY

Every five hundred years or so, Europe goes through a great and complex convulsion, when an inherited pattern breaks up and a new one emerges. The first century of our era, which saw the establishment both of the Roman Empire and of the Christian Church, was one. The end of the ancient world and the beginning of the Middle Ages in the fifth and sixth centuries was another. The schism between East and West, the end of the Viking era and the rise of the Papal Monarchy at the end of the first millennium formed yet another such complex; and the fall of Byzantium, the great discoveries, and the Renaissance and the Reformation formed another.

Now once more the pattern of nation states in Europe and the pattern of church life developed at the time of the Reformation and the Counter-Reformation are both breaking up. So are the patterns of thought which went with them. People are confused by change; and if they feel overwhelmed by change, which they cannot understand, they fall back into the few certainties they think they do understand. Unfortunately the only one which is widespread now is the kind of narrow nationalism which led to the disasters and catastrophes of two world wars in the twentieth century.

At each of the four previous crises, Christian thinkers emerged to help people to interpret what was happening, not passively as fate but actively as part of God's providence. Paul and the other New Testament writers in the first century and the Greek and Latin fathers in the patristic period, these all did their work of interpretation in a unifying way. By contrast, the crises of a thousand years ago and five hundred years ago led to the fragmentation of the church. It is a challenge to the churches, which have been the victims and the perpetrators of so much disunity, to work together now to accompany their peoples and nations into the third millennium with a message of peace, hope and unity.

More than anything we need now the moral perception to see what attitudes, what behaviour, what structures of church and state, what hopes and fears belong to the past and need to be discarded, and what belong to the future. Then we need to internalise a kind of moral ratchet to stop ourselves from slipping back. The Christian claim is that the things concerning Jesus belong to the future, which we have to move towards, even if it is true that he came to us in the past two thousand years ago. But there is no future in looking back; and where Christian churches confuse tradition, which is the means of conveying through the ages the good news of Jesus Christ, with traditionalism, with living in the past as though that is where we belong, then they sell people short. The late Metropolitan Anthony Bloom used to say that tradition is the living faith of dead people, and traditionalism is the dead faith of living people.

We mislead ourselves by singing carols containing phrases like 'long, long ago'. Two thousand is not a large number, and two thousand years is not a long period of time. I find it helpful to suppose that the earth will last for several billion years or so, if we look after it, and to remember that Jesus promised that the gates of hell would not prevail against the church. That means we are living in the early years of the church and that much is still in process of formation. It is an illusion to think that everything was settled with the compilation of the New Testament in the first century, or with the development of the creeds, the sacraments and the ministry in the second and third centuries, or by the great councils and missionary expansion of the church in the fourth and fifth centuries, and that all we have to do is to go on repeating what was formulated then.

The best lesson we can learn from those centuries is not how to gel or get stuck but how to cope with change, trusting in the promises of Jesus and the guidance of the Holy Spirit. We are part of early church history and the troubles, controversies, even schisms, which we presently experience, will one day be merely footnotes in doctoral theses. We are followers of one who did not say, 'I make all things old,' but 'I am making all things new' (Revelation 21:5).

> Then I saw a new heaven and a new earth; for the first heaven and the first earth had passed away, and the sea was no more. And I saw the holy city, the new Jerusalem, coming down out of heaven from God, prepared as a bride adorned for her husband. And I heard a loud voice from the throne saying,
>
>> 'See, the home of God is among mortals.
>> He will dwell with them as their God;
>> they will be his peoples,
>> and God himself will be with them;
>> he will wipe every tear from their eyes.
>> Death will be no more;
>> mourning and crying and pain will be no more,
>> for the first things have passed away.'
>
> And the one who was seated on the throne said, 'See, I am making all things new' ...
>
> Then the angel showed me the river of the water of life, bright as crystal, flowing from the throne of God and of the Lamb through the middle of the street of the city. On either side of the river is the tree of life with its twelve kinds of fruit, producing its fruit each month; and the leaves of the tree are for the healing of the nations. (Revelation 21:1–5; 22:1–2)

The story of humankind under God, as told in the Bible, begins in a garden, but it ends in a city. And that means that history and civilisation are to be taken seriously, and so are architecture and town planning and politics, which, after all, simply means the way in which citizens live together in a city or *polis*. God cares about all these things; they are not just painted scenery on a stage set for the dramas of the individual heart. It is this vision of the city in the very last chapter of the Bible which gives us the confidence after the victory of Christ on the cross to believe that the story of humankind since Adam has a meaning and is not merely, as Macbeth in his madness feared, 'a tale told by an idiot, full of sound and fury, signifying nothing'.[2] It gives us hope that while there is no way back to Eden, because an angel with a flaming sword stands at the gate, there is a way forward, where Christ has already gone, and that way is the way out of isolated individualism into an ordered community.

The actual life of cities, starting with Jericho in 20,000 BC and including Athens, Corinth, Rome and Jerusalem at the time of our Lord, has been sufficiently disgusting to lead many of those who could afford to do so to seek a rural retreat. Even Jesus had to set his face to leave 'the Sabbath rest of Galilee, the calm of hills above', to go to Jerusalem; but he did so in obedience to his Father's will. He went to the city to finish there the work the Father had given him to do.

The Industrial Revolution, particularly in England from which it spread to the rest of the world, changed the nature of cities and produced urban misery on such a scale that it is not surprising that writers like Rousseau, Wordsworth and Tolstoy should have encouraged a flight of the mind 'back to nature' and to an unobtainable innocence. It was always romantic intellectuals who thought that salvation could be found by going back to the land; peasants only want to leave it and press on into the city.

It is not a necessary part of discipleship that we should all live in cottages on the edge of national parks. It is the gospel that we should humanise Mumbai, Sheffield, Shanghai, Sao Paulo, Nairobi, Calcutta, Mexico City and all those cities where for millions the future of humankind lies.

The heavenly city, new Jerusalem, will not be an impersonal place. It is described as a bride adorned for her husband; so it will be personal and relational, not isolated and individual. Nor will God be. His dwelling place will be with men and women and they will be his people, or rather, as many of the old texts say, they will be his peoples and God himself will be with them. Nowhere in the Bible does the phrase occur, 'God with me'; it is always 'Immanuel, God with us'. No creed claims that Christ died for me; always Christ died for us. And that is not surprising, because salvation includes release from isolation and re-settlement in community. That is the perfectly good reason why so many people are converted to faith in Christ in late adolescence, when the loneliness of being a separate individual is experienced so intensely.

Actually, I do believe, in a quite straightforward and uncomplicated way, that Christ died for me and I claim for myself, as I suppose we all do, the standard mistranslation of the words of Job, 'I know that my Redeemer lives' (Job 19:25). Every Lent and Holy Week gives us an opportunity to appropriate, to make our own, this astonishing fact of our redemption. But it gives us the opportunity, once we have absorbed what it means to say 'Christ died for me', to go on to see that it must mean that he died for us, that he died for the whole nation, as Caiaphas accidentally prophesied; indeed, that he died for the nations, for the whole inhabited world, as the apostles proclaimed.

There is something to look forward to as an antidote to all those things we have to look back on. It is in the city, not in the garden, that death shall be no more. When David Jenkins became

Bishop of Durham in 1984 he realised that one of the things which had, as he said, 'gone dead' for many people and which needed re-vivifying was traditional Christian language. He took this as a challenge to produce two short 'mini-creeds' in modern language. The first reads: 'God is. He is as he is in Jesus. So there is hope.'[3] He was pleased that it is only thirteen words long and that, with the exception of the word *Jesus*, which he couldn't do anything about, it was entirely in words of one syllable. The fascinating thing is that in limiting himself to the choice of only one of the three theological virtues – the things which abide forever, faith, hope and love – he should have chosen hope to be the chief. St Paul, as is well known, chose love. For much of Christian history our leaders, by implication at least, have chosen faith. But I think that David Jenkins was right, like Jürgen Moltmann, at the end of the twentieth century, to concentrate on hope.

John in his Revelation encourages us to believe that there is hope for the nations too; but first there is judgement, for Jesus said in his last recorded parable:

> When the Son of Man comes in his glory, and all the angels with him, then he will sit on the throne of his glory. All the nations will be gathered before him, and he will separate people one from another as a shepherd separates the sheep from the goats, and he will put the sheep at his right hand and the goats at the left. Then the king will say to those at his right hand, 'Come, you that are blessed by my Father, inherit the kingdom prepared for you from the foundation of the world; for I was hungry and you gave me food, I was thirsty and you gave me something to drink' ... [and so on]. (Matthew 25:31–46)

The clue to the meaning of this well-known parable of the sheep and the goats is given in the introductory section: 'All the nations will be gathered before him'. This is not a parable about dipping into your pocket and giving to Christian Aid, though there are of course other very good reasons why you should do so. This is a parable of judgement, not so much on individuals as on nations.

We have seen how modern developments have made it easier for us to understand the fall, the whole creation groaning while it waits for us to be truly human (Romans 8:18–25). Now we can see that, whereas in earlier ages the only way to make sense of this parable was to turn it into an appeal to individuals and a prescription for individual behaviour, it can also be seen as a judgement on the nations and a description of the actual state of affairs which we see on television newsreels every night.

> 'I was hungry and you gave me no food, I was thirsty and you gave me nothing to drink, I was a stranger and you did not welcome me, naked and you did not give me clothing, sick and in prison and you did not visit me' …. 'Truly I tell you, just as you did not do it to one of the least of these, you did not do it to me.' And these will go away into eternal punishment, but the righteous into eternal life. (Matthew 25:42–46)

How does it stand with us, as a nation, in the heat and light of this judgement?

The eternal life of which the parable speaks will be lived in a city, a city in the midst of which there is a Lamb, standing as if it had been slain. 'I saw no temple in the city, for its temple is the Lord God the Almighty and the Lamb … the glory of God is its light, and its lamp is the Lamb. The nations will walk by its light … People will bring into it the glory and the honour of the nations' (Revelation 21:22–24). Although there is no temple, no church or churches, in the heavenly city, there are still nations and even, especially after his sacrifice of himself, Jesus the Lamb of God. No churches, only the nations and Jesus.

Other empires have taken as their emblem symbols of power and invincible might, the lion or the eagle or the bear; only this empire will be led by a Lamb. John holds before us this vision of a future international community in which distinction and difference and national characteristics will not be done away but will come together in amity and harmony under God.

And this cosmopolitan conurbation will not be a loathsome, traffic-clogged slum but a garden city dissected by a stream of pure water with a tree on either side. It is a fabulous tree, the stuff of which dreams are made, for among other things it is on both sides of the river at once. It is our old friend the tree of life, mentioned in the story of the Garden of Eden, but soon overshadowed by the dramatic glamour of the tree of the knowledge of good and evil. God drives Adam and Eve away from it; and it is to guard the way to it that he sets the angel with the flaming sword at the gate.

The tree of life drops out of the long story; but God has preserved it, as he preserved Joseph in Egypt and kept him safe there so that he in turn could preserve the life of his brothers. It is a tree which is never bare or in flower but always bearing fruit. I like to think that nine of its twelve annual crops are the fruit of the Spirit: love, joy, peace, patience, kindness, generosity, faithfulness, gentleness, self-control (Galatians 5:22–23); after all there is no law against such things. Then the other three fruits surpass our expectations, our imaginations and perhaps even our vocabulary. There are no words to describe the good things which God has in store for those who love him. But we may assume that they include health and salvation, and to that the tree of life bears witness in the last new image in the whole of Scripture, 'the leaves of the tree are for the healing of the nations'.

One of the many reasons why we should think twice before destroying tropical trees is that their leaves contain medicines, as yet undiscovered, which could help us all. Literally as well as symbolically, the leaves of trees are for the healing of the nations. For this reason, among others, I like to take literally the command to the angels of destruction 'Do not damage the earth or the sea or *the trees*' (Revelation 7:3, italics added). It is a positive word to our generation, to be taken together with the more negative and more terrifying, 'Your wrath has come, and the time for … destroying those who destroy the earth' (Revelation 11:18).

Whenever I walked across Prebend's Bridge over the gorge of the River Wear in Durham, I used to pause, look north and see 'a city and in the midst of the city a river, and on either side of the river, trees'. So far so good. But I also saw the cathedral; and I would recall that John had said, 'I saw no temple in the city, for its temple is the Lord God the Almighty and the Lamb.' I would remind myself that, for all that Dr Johnson had said to Boswell that Durham Cathedral gave 'an impression of rocky solidity and indeterminate duration', our sumptuous church was not one of those things which endure forever and which are destined to be given up to the Father by the Son at the end. Rather, as Prospero, speaking for Shakespeare, knew:

> *The cloud-capp'd towers, the gorgeous palaces*
> *The solemn temples, the great globe itself*
> *Yea, all which it inherit shall dissolve.*
> *And like this insubstantial pageant faded,*
> *Leave not a rack behind.*
> *We are such stuff as dreams are made on;*
> *And our little life is rounded with a sleep.*[4]

QUESTIONS

1. What lessons can we draw from the constant misrepresentation of Mary Magdalene?

2. What makes you weep? What are you looking for?

3. What are the implications of regarding ourselves as 'part of early church history'?

4. Produce a short, simple creed to rival that of David Jenkins.

5. What are the ecological implications of the book of Revelation?